Cooking With Style

Junior Auxiliary of
Biloxi - Ocean Springs,
Mississippi

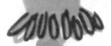

Junior Auxiliary Prayer

Send us, O God, as Thy messengers to the hearts without a home, to lives without love, to the crowds without a guide. Send us to the children whom none have blessed, to the famished whom none have visited, to the fallen whom none have lifted, to the bereaved whom none have comforted.

Kindle Thy flame on the altars of our hearts, that others may be warmed thereby; cause Thy light to shine in our souls, that others may see the way; keep our sympathies and insight ready, our wills keen, our hands quick to help others in their need.

Grant us clear vision, true judgment, with great daring as we seek to right the wrong; and so endow us with cheerful love that we may minister to the suffering and forlorn even as Thou wouldst. May the blessing of God Almighty, the Father, the Son, and the Holy Spirit, rest upon us and upon all our work. May He give us light to guide us, courage to support us, and love to unite us now and forever more.

Amen.

All proceeds benefit
The Junior Auxiliary of Biloxi-Ocean Springs.

WIMMER
COOKBOOKS

A CONSOLIDATED GRAPHICS COMPANY

800.548.2537   wimmerco.com

The Junior Auxiliary of Biloxi-Ocean Springs Junior Auxiliary, was established in 1965 and became a charter member of the National Association of Junior Auxiliaries, headquartered in Greenville, Mississippi.

Today, the organization has 63 active members and 137 life and associate members who contribute volunteer hours to service projects, health care, welfare and fundraising. The organization provides basic needs including food and clothing to less fortunate children in Biloxi, Ocean Springs and the surrounding areas. Other activities include educating children in dental hygiene, stranger danger, bully proofing and basic etiquette, and assists young teenage mothers with both moral and financial support.

Profits from sales of this cookbook will be used to fund the organization's many projects and programs. We wish to thank everyone who contributed to this endeavor especially those who submitted recipes. We are not listing those names because many were lost in Hurricane Katrina. And we thank *you* for helping us by purchasing a copy of our cookbook.

Junior Auxiliary of Biloxi-Ocean Springs
Executive Board
2006-2007

Kristi Davis	President
Sharon Weeks	Vice President
Jennifer Schmidt	Treasurer
Sarah Rimes	Recording Secretary
Courtney Denton	Corresponding Secretary
Dana Mitchell	Parliamentarian
Anne Anderson	Finance Chairperson
Deborah Migues	Projects Chairperson

The artwork of *Cooking With Style* has been provided by Shelby Brune.

Active Members

Joanna Allen
Anne Anderson
Kala Bowen
Angela Bull
Amy Cochran
Karen Cole
Patricia Collins
Julie Cruthirds
Kristi Davis
Courtney Denton
Lori Derouen
April Descher
Meredith Descher
Kristen Dibble
Bethany Dill
Julie Eustice
Alison Felsher
Sara Gammill
Jody Grimes
Anna Harris
Leslie Hensarling
Leslie Heard
Stacey Johnson
Anna Kalom
Robin LaGrone
Stephanie Lamppin-Chen
Marie Lee
Amy Lemon
Ashley Lott
Debbie Luber
Hannah Mayfield
Jenny McArthur
Jami McCollough
Mindy McDowell
Shelley McKay

Deborah Migues
Dana Mitchell
Celeste Oglesby
Renee Pennell
Elisa Radich
Kelly Rhodes
Sarah Rimes
Rhonda Roberts
Eden Rubenstein
Lynn Rush
Adrienne Sawyer
Jennifer Schmidt
Julie Schmidt
Stephanie Schmitt
Julie Scruggs
Stephanie Seymour
Wendy Snyder
Karla Steckler
Carrie Stewart
Jon'elle Swetman
Terri Tomsik
Sharon Weeks
Jennifer Whitney
Brenda Whitwell
Rebecca Wicht
Marie Williams

Life Members

Judy Holmes Abide
Patricia Guntey Adkins
Sharon Neirynck Travis
Gaye Smith Aultman
Gail Holden Banks
Kristin Swendsen Bates
Lucia Osmondson Baublits
Brenda Hailey Baumeister

Mary Marr Dunlop Beckman
Marcia Nick Blevens
Priscilla Ober Bolton
Margaret Butte Booth
Joanna Marshall Bosco
Ann Phillips Boyd
Linda Dalgo Bradford
Brenda Boyce Branch
Linden Bourgeois Brashier
Rhonda McNair Breland
Barbara Hilbert Brewer
Christi Hager Brietzke
Sylvia Davidson Briscoe
Carol Adams Burdick
Mary Anne Maxwell Caldwell
Martha Gayle Peeler Ceasar
Lisa Hale Chapman
Deidra Colson
Gloria Bossier Compton
Margaret Dore Compton
Phyllis Lawton Consentino
Jo Boyd Corban
Marty Haney Dees
Renee McDonald Dellenger
Lucy Connor Denton
Kay Tubbs Dew
Mildred Green Dickson
Alys Taylor Donovan
Debbie Johnson Drake
Ann Charlton Duke
Laura Cuicchi Endt
Rita Schweickert Endt
Maria Hernandez Erickson
Rosina Fritz Feeney

Michelle Catchot Fillipich

Cindy Burgess Ford

Merileigh Miner Furr

Jean Inglis Garner

Mary Lee Williams
    Garrand

Nancy Joachim Gollott

Gigi Gould

Madelon Reid Gruich

Ann Fink Guice

Dottye Langhofer Gunn

Hope Sullivan Hamilton

Jan Dubuisson Hamilton

Jane Sheely Hamilton

Sharon Finley Harper

Ginger Coley Harrison

Nora Stevens Harvey

Gene Helm Hodges

Judy King Hudson

Lee Ann Hough Hunter

Debbie Dees Ivy

Elizabeth Corso Joachim

Sandy Taylor Johnson

Karen Stumpf Kasovich

Lori Pavlik Kelly

Sandra Casey Knight

Elaine Furstner Kotchmar

Christine Taft Krivanec

Rose Cook Kyle

Ann Beyrefitte LaRosa

Patricia Endt Latil

Nancy Neyman Lemon

Jeanne Carter Luckey

Ginger Carrington
    Magruder

Anna Tarczanin Martin

Barbara Herrin Mason

Dianne Luke Mattiace

Jeanne LaCour Mavar

Nancy Pierce Mavar

Sharon Mahon Maxey

Jane Tucker McElroy

Judy Webb Meyers

Kay Alexander Miller

Margaret Dowd Miller

Sylvia Flemming Minor

Kellie Smith Mitchell

Martha Howard Mohler

Ann Marie Miller Moreton

Sallie Baumhauer Noblin

Myra Sampson Olson

Kim Bunton Overstreet

Mary Ann Sadka Petro

Melissa Gallé Polk

Joanne Gay Pollina

Elizabeth Rahaim Ponder

Mary Rose Kettering Pott

Ann Slayden Pringle

Kay Rhineberger Pringle

Judy Sadler Rash

Carrie Wade Rester

Heather Donnelly
    Riemann

Debra Fayard Rogers

Virgina Kerth Roper

Mary Buyers Sablich

Mary Charles Cox Saucier

Cecilia Gollott Schmidt

Lucy Schwab Selman

Lynn Zickle Simnicht

Lisa McAllister Simons

Catherine Gaudet
    Sliman

Mary Agnes LeBlanc
    Sliman

Olivia Mavar Sliman

Beverly Michael Smith

Towana Brown Smith

Anna Lacy Stanfield

Susan Bowen Stanfield

Judy Shuff Steckler

Sue Lee Strangi

Patricia Staehle Striegel

Jane Gwaltney Sutton

Avis Vignes Switzer

Mary Hurd Terrell

Sue Gatewood Thomas

Judy Steward Thurman

Kelly Eldridge Tootle

Katie Soyars Tynes

Mary Sue May Veal

Kally Halkias Vlahos

Betty Sumrall Walker

Susan Sullivan Warren

Candice Vaughn Webb

Audrey Brandt
    Westbrook

Faye Owen Williams

Joyce Fountain Wiltz

Gaye Bush Winter

Associate Members

Karen Dibbs Brashier

Sustaining Members

Joyce Tyson Christian

Mary Alice Fairbank Miner

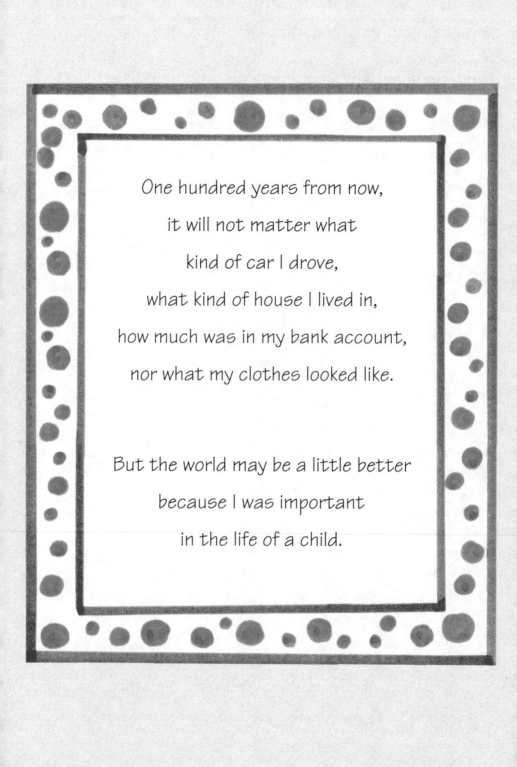

One hundred years from now,

it will not matter what

kind of car I drove,

what kind of house I lived in,

how much was in my bank account,

nor what my clothes looked like.

But the world may be a little better

because I was important

in the life of a child.

Tips on Etiquette and Style...

- Salad should be served between the entrée and the dessert. This is correct in spite of the custom in almost all restaurants of serving it as a first course. Or, it may be served with the entrée, on a separate salad plate.

- Wine glasses are filled only halfway, never to the top of the glass. If more than one wine is to be served during dinner, there should be a glass for each wine.

- Wine glasses should be picked up by the stem rather than the bowl. In the case of white wine and champagne this helps to keep the wine cool, and in the case of all wines, including red wines, it enables you to appreciate the color.

- The first piece to be put on the table, once the cloth is in place (if using one) is the centerpiece. As its name implies, it must be in the exact center. It must never be so high that the diners cannot see over it, but its length and width are limited only by the size of your table.

- Candles for the most formal dinner should be white, and brand new. Only if there is no evidence of smoke or drips, might a used candle be permissible. Candles are lighted before the guests come to the table and remain lighted until they leave the dining room.

- Displays of affection or attraction are often embarrassing to others, are not appropriate in the presence of children, and belong in a private setting. Holding hands, affectionate greetings accompanied by a kiss on the cheek, or a quick hug are perfectly acceptable in public. Passion is not.

- It is hard to understand why so many otherwise attractive people totally destroy their appearance by chewing gum like a cow chewing a cud. Chewing gum, in itself, if it is done quietly and unobtrusively, is not unattractive. But when one does it with grimaces, open mouth, smacks, crackles and pops, and worst of all with bubbles, it is in the worst of taste.

- There is no doubt that a person who stands and sits erect looks best. Graceful standing and walking posture includes the following components: shoulders back, chin in and slightly up, abdomen and stomach in, back straight, and knees relaxed.

- When departing a dinner party, once you have decided that it is time to go — GO! Nothing is more irritating than the guest who gets her coat, says good-bye to the other guests, and twenty minutes later is still standing in the open door giving last-minute words of wisdom to her hostess.

- At the end of a meal a woman may quickly powder her nose and put on a little lipstick, but to look in a mirror and daub at the face for any length of time is in bad taste.

- Don't wear an excessive amount of lipstick to the table, out of consideration for your hostess' napkin, and also because it is very unattractive on the rim of a glass or on the silver.

- Always wear your perfume or cologne sparingly!

- Anytime you serve punch, think outside the bowl. Use any large interesting food safe container for a punch bowl.

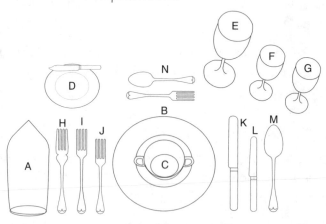

A: Napkin
B: Service Plate
C: Soup bowl on plate
D: Bread and butter plate
with butter knife

E: Water Glass
F: White wine
G: Red Wine
H: Fish fork
I: Dinner Fork

J: Salad fork
K: Service Knife
L: Fish knife
M: Soup spoon
N: Dessert spoon and
cake fork

- If you are using a buffet plate or charger try this for an extra special place setting. Condition small flowers and leaves in a small bowl of cold water. Drain and pat dry. Place dinner plate on charger and place flowers around the charger rim minutes before guests arrive.

- Seasonal fruits and vegetables make fabulous containers for fresh flowers and will add interest to your table.

- If you host a dinner party and use candles on your table be sure they are unscented. Unscented candles will not interfere with the flavors of your food.

- Never neglect color. It plays an important part in the enjoyment of food.

- Lining a basket for rolls:
  Spread a large square napkin, right side facing down, on a flat surface. Fold each of the four corners to meet exactly in the center. Preserve those folds and turn the napkin over to fold each corner to meet in the center again. Place in the basket, holding down the ends in the center. Bring each loose corner up from underneath. This makes a nest for your rolls and helps to keep them warm.

- To condition flowers, cut the ends of all stems at an angle. Remove any leaves that might be submerged in the final arrangement. Plunge the plant material into a bucket of water with three or four drops of bleach added. Leave in a cool light location for at least 8 hours. When you are ready, arrange flowers in your container of choice. Change the water regularly and be sure to add a drop or two of bleach each time.

- Allow 1 set of salt and pepper shakers for every six people.

- Cook with eggs that are at room temperature.

- When you are finished with your meal, simply place the fork and knife side-by-side (parallel) on the plate, either horizontally or diagonally (handles at either 3:00 or 4:00). The tines of the fork can be up or down, but generally when eating European style, the tines are down.

- Also, as a general rule, while you are eating and resting between bites, the handles of the fork or knife are not supposed to touch the table once used. Place the knife at the top of the plate with the sharp edge facing toward you.

- When finished with soup, the spoon should be placed on the accompanying saucer or plate.

- It is fine to take leftover food home from a restaurant. However, if you have eaten more than ½ the food on your plate, then it's best to not take the rest home. If more than ½ the food on your plate is left, the waiter should offer to "wrap it" for you without your asking. Instead of asking for a "doggy bag", if the waiter doesn't offer, then ask the waiter to "please wrap this for me".

- Diamonds in the daytime were once looked upon as improper. But, that was a long time ago, and is an outdated concept. As long as the diamonds are not elaborate, then go ahead and wear them anytime and anywhere you like.

- Timeless clothes include trench coats, turtleneck sweaters, pencil skirts and blazers.

- Develop your own sense of style. If you discover clothes that work, keep them.

- A v-neck shirt or sweater is flattering to all.

- If you want your neck to look longer and thinner, consider wearing an open neckline.

- Accessories are an affordable, easy way to update clothes.

- A set of gold/silver bangles goes with everything.

- A simple watch face on a black or brown leather band or on a metal band creates a timeless look.

- You cannot go wrong with either gold, pearl, or diamond studs. They go with anything.

- Save your splurges for great shoes, great bags, and excellent tailoring – they elevate your entire look.

- Keep leather skirts away from leather boots. Instead, try pumps or T-straps. If you want to wear boots with your leather skirt, go with a suede pair. The reverse works too, combine a suede skirt with leather boots, but skip the suede and suede combo.

- When you are wearing a straight skirt with boots, always reveal some leg in between, bare skin or dark tights, whatever you prefer. Closing up this space can make your legs look stumpy. When you show your legs – even only a couple of inches – the problem is solved. A flared or full skirt with boots can look right with no leg showing at all, as long as the boots are fitted through the ankle. One "boots-and-skirts" policy that applies across the board, the boot top should always fit snugly around your calf.

- When wearing a pencil skirt, you should be able to comfortably perform the basic motions of daily life – like walking and sitting. Do not buy a skirt that forces you to teeter in baby steps or to sit with your thighs glued together.

- It's easy to be careless about T-shirts, but a nice fit makes a huge difference. Choose tees that are tailored, rather than boxy, in not-too-thick fabrics. Cap sleeves work well on most figures, because they broaden the shoulders and make the waist look smaller. Avoid short sleeves that hit right in the middle of the upper arm and any sleeves that do not fit snugly. With long-sleeve tees, err on the side of extra length, with the hem of the sleeve hitting the heel of your hand.

- Do not wear a necklace with a sleek high-neck sweater. Instead, dress it up with long earrings. The same applies for boatnecks and turtlenecks.

- Putting a big chunk of your sweater budget toward a good cashmere sweater is better than owning a heap of mid-quality pieces. It's the one you will reach for time and time again.

- If you have to think about whether an outfit works, do not bother with it; dressing should be easy.

- If jeans stand away from your tailbone when you sit, or the waistband presses torturously into your lower belly, skip them. Do not buy an uncomfortable pair of jeans – no matter how good they look when you're standing.

- A suit is meant to look sharp. The vibe you are going for is clean and crisp. Your jacket should fit well through the shoulder and underarm. When closed, it should lie flat with no pulling across the chest or around the buttons. Pants should be fitted through the hip, but should never be very tight. The sleeve of the jacket should end at the heel of your hand.

- If you wear a button-down shirt with a suit, you have the collar-placement dilemma to deal with – but there is no wrong answer here. Wearing your collar outside your jacket is a little downtown; inside has a kind of sophisticated French feel.

- Do not try to save money when buying a suit. A suit is an important part of your wardrobe, and you want to be able to wear it for years. Buy the best quality suit you can afford – especially when it comes to classic styles.

- Always wear clothes that complement your body, regardless of trends; if you look great, that's all anyone's going to notice.

- Style means walking confidently and knowing you look good – not tugging at your dress or hiding your bra straps.

- When purchasing a clutch purse, make sure it has a little wrist strap. Without a strap, even something as simple as having a drink becomes an effort because your clutch always occupies one of your hands.

- When breaking in new shoes, wear them for a little while, then switch – do not wear them for two days in a row. And remember: It's not worth it to wear great new shoes when your feet are covered in bandages.

- To keep your bra invisible under clothing, do not match the color of the shirt; match the color of your skin.

- Don't buy anything on sale that you wouldn't consider at full price.

Table of Contents

Favorite Recipes from My Cookbook

Recipe Title	Page #

Appetizers

Dips, Spreads, Salsas,
Relishes, Sandwiches,
Cheese Balls, etc.

Artichoke and Spinach Tarts

1	package frozen puff pastry	1/2	cup mayonnaise
1	14-ounce can drained and mashed artichoke hearts	3/4	cup grated Parmesan cheese
1	10-ounce package frozen spinach	1	teaspoon onion powder
		3/4	teaspoon garlic powder

Preheat oven to 400°. Thaw pastry dough and roll out. Thaw spinach and drain well on paper towels. Mix all ingredients and spread mixture onto dough. Roll tightly, jelly-roll style and wrap in plastic wrap. Freeze at least 30 minutes. Slice and bake for approximately 10 minutes.

12 TO 15 SERVINGS.

● ● ● ● ● ● ● ● ● ● ● ● ● ● ●

Can be prepared ahead of time, freezes well

Bacon Swirls

1	8-ounce can crescent rolls	1	tablespoon minced onion
1	3-ounce package cream cheese, softened	1	teaspoon milk
5	bacon slices, cooked and crumbled		grated Parmesan cheese

Unroll crescent roll dough, and separate into four rectangles; press to seal. Mix cream cheese and next 3 ingredients. Spread mixture evenly over dough, then roll, pressing edges to seal. Cut each roll into 8 slices, and place on ungreased baking sheet. Sprinkle with Parmesan. Bake for 12 to 15 minutes or until lightly browned. Serve warm.

Appetizers

Bacon Tomato Appetizer

1	cup mayonnaise	1	pound bacon, crumbled
1	cup sour cream	2	large tomatoes, chopped

Combine mayonnaise, sour cream, and half of bacon. Mix well. Refrigerate until serving time. When ready to serve top with remaining bacon and tomatoes. Serve with bagel chips.

Bacon Wraps

1	large can whole water chestnuts	Worcestershire sauce
1	pound sliced bacon	toothpicks

Cut water chestnuts in half and soak in Worcestershire sauce 1½ hours. Cut sliced bacon in three pieces and wrap one piece around each water chestnut. Stick with toothpick to hold. Bake until bacon is crisp at 375°.

Baked Cream Cheese

1	can crescent rolls	½	teaspoon dill weed
1	8-ounce package cream cheese	1	beaten egg yolk

Sprinkle cream cheese with dill weed and wrap with crescent rolls. Brush lightly with beaten egg. Bake at 350° for 15 minutes or until golden brown.

• • • • • • • • • • • • • • • •

Can substitute Brie cheese and rosemary.

Appetizers

Baked Artichoke Dip

1   14-ounce can marinated
    artichoke hearts
1   cup mayonnaise
1   cup grated Parmesan cheese

1   teaspoon garlic powder
1   teaspoon salt
1   teaspoon lemon juice

Drain artichokes well. Squeeze out all the juice. Cut artichokes into small pieces and add mayonnaise and Parmesan cheese. Mix well. Add garlic powder and salt, mix lightly. Place in a shallow baking dish, suitable for serving dip, and bake at 350° for approximately 20 minutes or until brown on top. Serve with corn chips or Melba toast rounds.

Black Bean and Corn Salsa

1   16-ounce can black beans,
    drained and rinsed
1   cup kernel corn
½   cup red bell pepper, chopped
½   cup cilantro, chopped
    bunch green onions, sliced

2   tablespoons balsamic vinegar
½   teaspoon cumin
3   teaspoons extra virgin olive oil
1   teaspoon garlic, or to taste
    pinch of salt and pepper
    juice of 1 lime

Combine all ingredients, mix well. Store covered in the refrigerator for up to 3 days. Serve with tortilla chips.

Appetizers

Black-Eyed Pea Salsa

1   15-ounce can black-eyed peas,
        drained and rinsed
½   cup chopped celery
¼   cup chopped red onion
1   tablespoon chopped cilantro

¼   cup red wine vinegar
1   tablespoon olive oil
1   teaspoon sugar
        salt and pepper, to taste

Toss black-eyed peas, celery, onion and cilantro in a medium bowl. Mix vinegar, oil, sugar, and salt and pepper in another bowl. Pour over black-eyed pea mixture and toss gently until well coated.

Brie Kisses

⅔   pound Brie cheese
1   17.3-ounce package frozen puff
        pastry

red and green pepper jelly

Cut Brie into 32 half-inch cubes and arrange on a plate. Place in freezer. Let pastry thaw at room temperature for 30 minutes; unfold each pastry and roll with a rolling pin to remove creases. Slice each sheet into quarters and slice each quarter into half. Cut each piece in half one more time for a total of 32 squares. Place squares into greased mini-muffin cups; arrange so corners of dough point upwards. Bake at 400° for 5 minutes. Place one Brie cube in center of each pastry. Bake 10 minutes or until the edges are golden. Remove from pan and top with pepper jelly. Serve immediately.

32 SERVINGS.

BLT Bites

20 cherry tomatoes
1 pound bacon, cooked and crumbled
½ cup mayonnaise or salad dressing

⅓ cup chopped green peppers
3 tablespoons grated Parmesan cheese
2 tablespoons snipped fresh parsley

Cut a thin slice off each tomato top. Scoop out and discard pulp. Invert the tomato on a paper towel to drain. In a small bowl, combine remaining ingredients; mix well. Spoon mixture into tomatoes. Refrigerate for several hours.

16 TO 20 SERVINGS.

BLT Dip

2 cups sour cream
6 plum tomatoes, chopped
2 cups mayonnaise or salad dressing

3 green onions, chopped
2 pounds sliced bacon, cooked and crumbled
assorted crackers or chips

In a bowl, combine the sour cream, mayonnaise, bacon, tomatoes and onions. Refrigerate until serving. Serve with crackers or chips.

6 CUPS.

Appetizers

Broiled Crab Meltaways

6	English muffin halves	1	4.5-ounce can crabmeat, drained
1/4	pound margarine	1	6-ounce jar old English sharp Cheddar cheese spread
2	tablespoons mayonnaise		
1/2	teaspoon garlic salt	1/2	teaspoon seasoned salt

Cut muffins into quarters. Mix remaining ingredients and spread on muffins. Freeze at least 20 minutes (may be kept in freezer for weeks). Bake or broil until puffy and brown. Serve hot.

Brushetta

2	large scallions	2	cups Roma tomatoes, peeled and diced
1/3	cup feta cheese		
1	tablespoon olive oil	2	teaspoons balsamic vinegar
2	tablespoons chives		garlic butter

In a small skillet, cook onions in oil until soft. Stir in tomatoes and salt and pepper to taste. Cook for 1 minute or until heated thoroughly. In a bowl, toss tomato mixture, cheese, chives, and vinegar. Mound about 1 tablespoon on seasoned side of toast.

Toast: Cut French bread into slices. Rub with garlic butter. Toast in oven or broil until crunchy.

Appetizers

Cheddar and Spinach Bar

1 cup all-purpose flour	1 package frozen chopped spinach, drained
1 teaspoon baking powder	
1 pound sharp Cheddar cheese, grated	1 cup whole milk
	¼ cup butter
2 eggs beaten	½ cup chopped onion

Add eggs to milk. Add butter, flour, and remaining ingredients. Stir and pour into a 6x9-inch baking dish. Bake at 350° for approximately 30 minutes or until brown on top.

Cool and cut into squares.

Cheese Ball

2 cups shredded mild Cheddar cheese	½ bunch chopped green onions
	1 cup mayonnaise
2 cups shredded sharp Cheddar cheese	1 cup chopped pecans
	1 10½-ounce jar strawberry preserves
1 teaspoon cayenne pepper	

Mix all ingredients except pecans and preserves. Form into a ball and roll over pecans. Let sit for 4 to 5 hours or overnight. Top with strawberry preserves prior to serving.

● ● ● ● ● ● ● ● ● ● ● ● ● ●

This makes enough for 2 balls and can be frozen without preserves.

Cheese Ball with Chopped Beef

1   8-ounce package cream cheese,
    softened
2   teaspoons grated onion
3   teaspoons prepared horseradish

4   drops hot sauce
1   jar chopped beef
    chopped nuts

Mix all ingredients except nuts and roll into a ball. Refrigerate. Before serving, roll ball in chopped nuts. Let stand at room temperature about an hour before serving

Cheese Coins

8   ounces shredded sharp Cheddar
    cheese
1   tablespoon Worcestershire
    sauce
½   cup butter or margarine,
    softened

2   tablespoons instant minced
    onion
1   cup flour
    sesame seeds, optional
    pinch of Cayenne pepper,
    optional

Mix all ingredients, except sesame seeds, in a medium bowl. Stir until dough forms. Divide dough in half and roll each half into a log, 1-inch in diameter, and 12 inches long. Roll logs in sesame seeds if desired. Wrap each log in plastic wrap and chill several hours to overnight. Carefully cut logs crosswise into 1/4-inch slices. Place on a greased and floured baking sheet. Bake at 375° for 10 to 12 minutes or until light brown. These must be watched because it is easy to overcook them. Using a metal spatula or pancake turner, remove coins from the baking sheet and cool on wire racks. Coins may be stored in airtight container to be kept crunchy.

84 COINS.

Cheese Straws

2	sticks margarine	2½	cups all-purpose flour
1	12-ounce package extra sharp Cheddar cheese grated	1	teaspoon red pepper
		1	teaspoon salt

Cream margarine and cheese; add flour, pepper and salt. Use star attachment of cookie press and squeeze into straws the length of the cookie sheet. Bake at 350° until barely brown. (Under done = not crisp; Too brown = off taste) Break into lengths about 4 inches long. Shorter or longer is O.K, since they often break where they want!

Crab Mornay

½	stick butter	¼	pound Swiss cheese, shredded
½	bunch green onions, chopped	2	tablespoons white wine
¼	cup chopped fresh parsley	1	6½-ounce container crabmeat
	salt and pepper, to taste	1	6-ounce package fresh mushrooms, sliced
1	tablespoon flour		red pepper, to taste
1	cup milk		

Sauté green onions and parsley in butter. Simmer for a few minutes until onions are tender. Season to taste with salt, black and red pepper. Stir in flour, milk, and Swiss cheese; add wine and crabmeat. Simmer until ready to serve. Add mushrooms to Crab Mornay 15 minutes before serving. Serve on buttered toast or use as a hot dip with crackers.

Corn Dip

½   cup sour cream
½   cup mayonnaise
1   11-ounce can Mexican corn

2   cups cream cheese
     chopped chives

Mix all ingredients together and serve with corn chips.

Crab Puffs

2   sticks margarine
2   jars Old English cheese spread
1   tablespoon mayonnaise

     garlic and salt to taste
1   pound lump crabmeat
2   packages English muffins

Combine all ingredients. Spread a generous layer on ½ English muffin. Bake at 350° for 10 to 15 minutes until bubbly.

Crabmeat Dip

1   8-ounce package cream cheese
1   stick of butter
1   pound lump crabmeat
1   small onion, finely chopped

1   garlic toe, minced
     dash hot pepper sauce
     dash red pepper

Melt cheese and butter in a double boiler. Sift through crabmeat for shells; add crabmeat and remaining ingredients to butter mixture. Serve with Melba rounds in a chaffing dish.

8 TO 10 SERVINGS.

• • • • • • • • • • • • • • •

Can be prepared ahead of time

Appetizers

Cranberry Pineapple Relish

1	16-ounce can whole-berry cranberry sauce	2	tablespoons orange juice
1	8-ounce can pineapple tidbits, drained	2	tablespoons honey
		½	teaspoon ground ginger

In a small saucepan over medium low heat on stovetop, combine cranberry sauce, pineapple juice and orange juice. Cook for approximately 20 minutes, stirring occasionally. Remove from heat. Stir in honey and ginger.

Cucumber Sandwiches

Filling

1 8-ounce package cream cheese

¾ cup minced finely chopped Vidalia onion or to taste

½ teaspoon dill weed, to taste

salt and pepper, to taste, make a little peppery

1 medium cucumber grated by hand and drained well, between paper towels

Bread Preparations

1 tub whipped butter

4 loaves Pepperidge Farm bread

1 cucumber for garnish sliced thin and then cut into fourths

fresh dill, use a small piece to garnish

From each slice of bread cut 2 medallion-sized shapes, spread with butter, then cucumber mixture. Garnish with ¼ slice of cucumber and dill. Store in box covered with damp paper towels completely airtight. A biscuit cutter works well to cut the bread into medallions.

Appetizers

Crawfish Dip

5	tablespoons margarine	1	can golden mushroom soup
1	medium onion, finely chopped	1	roll garlic cheese
2	ribs celery, chopped		red pepper, to taste
2	pounds crawfish tails		minced parsley, to taste

Sauté onion and celery in margarine. Add crawfish tails and cook 20 minutes. Add mushroom soup and garlic cheese. Mix together. Place mixture in chaffing dish and serve with Melba rounds.

● ● ● ● ● ● ● ● ● ● ● ● ● ● ●

This dip may be served in heated patty shells.

Easy Cheesy Ball

2	8-ounce packages cream cheese, softened	1	envelope ranch dressing mix
1	8-ounce package shredded sharp Cheddar cheese	1/4	teaspoon hot pepper sauce
		1	10-ounce package chopped pecans

Combine cream cheese, Cheddar cheese, dressing mix and hot pepper sauce; form into a ball. Roll ball in chopped pecans to cover. Refrigerate overnight before serving.

12 SERVINGS.

Appetizers

Giblet Gravy

3	cups chicken broth	4	boiled eggs, chopped
	finely chopped liver and gizzard	3	tablespoons dressing
½	cup finely chopped green onions		salt and pepper, to taste

Wash and remove giblets from hen or turkey. Sauté liver, gizzard and onions in broth until tender. Add chopped boiled eggs, dressing and salt and pepper.

Glazed Bacon

1	pound sliced bacon	1	cup packed brown sugar
¼	cup orange juice	2	tablespoons Dijon mustard

Place bacon on a rack in an ungreased 15x10x1-inch baking pan. Bake at 350° for 10 minutes; drain. Combine brown sugar, orange juice and mustard; pour half over bacon. Bake for another 10 minutes. Turn bacon and drizzle with remaining glaze. Bake 15 minutes longer or until golden brown. Place bacon on waxed paper until set. Serve warm.

Good For You Guacamole

3	avocados	1	tomato
1	8-ounce container low-fat cottage cheese	1	red onion
			Juice of 1 lemon

Chop avocados, tomato, and onion. Mix together with cottage cheese and lemon juice. Serve with tortilla chips.

Appetizers

Greek Salad Dip

1 package miniature pita bread

Spread

2	8-ounce packages cream cheese, room temperature	1	teaspoon dried oregano
6	ounces feta cheese	¼	teaspoon Cayenne pepper
¼	cup sour cream	2	cloves garlic, minced

Toppings

1	small chopped tomato	½	small cucumber, seeded and chopped
3	chopped green onions		Greek olives halves

Combine spread ingredients with a mixer or food processor. Place spread in shallow glass dish and sprinkle with toppings. Make a ring of Greek olive halves around outside edge. Serve with miniature pita bread cut in halves or thirds.

Ham Rolls

2	packages dinner rolls in aluminum pan	2	tablespoons mustard
1	pound shaved deli ham	1½	sticks margarine, melted
½	pound sliced American cheese	1	tablespoon Worcestershire sauce
3	tablespoons poppy seeds		

Melt margarine, stir in poppy seeds, mustard, and Worcestershire sauce. Slice rolls in half horizontally. Layer ham and cheese inside rolls. Brush tops of rolls with butter and seasoning mixture. Heat in oven until the cheese is melted. Cut rolls along lines and serve.

Appetizers

Herb Mushroom Pâté

6	cups sliced fresh mushrooms	1	teaspoon crushed dried thyme
1	clove garlic minced	1/8	teaspoon crushed dried rosemary
3	tablespoons butter		
1	8-ounce package cream cheese, softened	1	teaspoon pepper
2	tablespoons dry sherry	1	teaspoon lemon-pepper seasoning
1	teaspoon crushed dried tarragon		salt to taste
1	teaspoon crushed dried marjoram		assorted crackers

In a 12-inch skillet, cook mushrooms and garlic in butter about 5 minutes, Cool to room temperature. In a food processor bowl, combine mushroom mixture, cream cheese, sherry, tarragon, marjoram, thyme, rosemary, pepper, lemon-pepper seasoning, and salt. Process until smooth. Brush a 3 cup mold with cooking oil. Transfer mushroom mixture to mold. Cover and chill 8 hours. Unmold on to a serving plate. Garnish with fresh mushrooms and serve with assorted crackers.

Homemade Salsa

1	jar of medium salsa	1/2	small can fine chopped olives, optional
1	can Rotel tomatoes, drained		
1	8-ounce bottle Italian dressing	1	package shredded Monterey Jack and Colby Jack cheese

Mix and chill. Serve with chips.

Hot Artichoke Dip

2	14-ounce cans drained artichoke hearts	1	tablespoon crushed garlic
1	cup grated Parmesan cheese	½	lemon, juiced
1	cup mayonnaise		dash paprika
			dash hot sauce, to taste

Preheat over to 350°. Mash artichoke hearts and mix with remaining ingredients. Bake in oven for approximately 25 minutes until warm and cheese is melted.

10 TO 12 SERVINGS.

Can be prepared ahead of time but does not freeze well.

Hot Artichoke and Spinach Dressing with Lump Crabmeat

⅔	cup mayonnaise	1	14-ounce can artichoke hearts, drained and coarsely chopped
¼	cup Parmesan cheese		
¼	cup Romano cheese	½	cup chopped spinach, frozen is fine
1	clove (fresh) garlic, finely minced		
¼	teaspoon basil	½	cup lump crabmeat
¼	teaspoon garlic salt	¼	cup grated mozzarella cheese
1	8-ounce package cream cheese (room temperature)		salt and pepper, to taste

Cream together mayonnaise, Parmesan, Romano, garlic, basil, garlic salt and cream cheese. Mix well. Add the artichokes hearts, spinach, and lump crabmeat. Mix well. Spray a pie pan with Pam, pour in dip, and top with mozzarella cheese. Bake at 350° for 20 to 25 minutes or until the top is browned. Serve with toasted bread.

Appetizers

Hot Chicken Wing Dip

4   chicken breasts, cooked
         and shredded
         (can use precooked chicken)
1/2-3/4 jar chicken wing sauce –
         medium or hotter

2½ cups mozzarella cheese
1   8-ounce package cream cheese
1   cup blue cheese dressing,
         optional

Spread cream cheese in a 9x13-inch pan. Heat chicken and wing sauce in the microwave until hot. Add ½ cup mozzarella cheese. Spread chicken mixture over cream cheese, then spread the blue cheese over chicken mixture; add all but ½ cup cheese and bake at 350° for 20 to 25 minutes until bubbly. Sprinkle rest of cheese on top. Serve with tortilla chips, celery, or whatever you like.

Hot Crab Dip

1   6-ounce can white crabmeat,
         drained
2   8-ounce packages cream cheese
1/4   cup mayonnaise
1   tablespoon confectioners' sugar

3   tablespoons white wine
1/2   teaspoon salt
1/2   teaspoon onion juice
1/2   teaspoon dry mustard
1/4   teaspoon garlic powder

Preheat over to 375°. Let cream cheese soften before mixing. Combine all ingredients except crab. Add crabmeat last and mix to a smooth consistency. Bake in oven for 45 minutes, top will brown at end. Serve with Ritz crackers.

Hot Crabmeat and Artichoke Dip

1   8-ounce package cream cheese
1   cup mayonnaise
1   teaspoon chopped garlic
1   14-ounce can artichoke hearts in
    water, drained and chopped

1   cup shredded Cheddar cheese
1/3 cup sliced green onions
    (or yellow onion, finely chopped)
1-2 cups chopped imitation
    crabmeat

Preheat oven to 350°. Combine the cream cheese and mayonnaise. Add the garlic and the chopped artichokes, crabmeat, onions, and the shredded cheese. Mix well. Spoon into an 8x8-inch square baking dish or an 8x11-inch oblong baking dish. Bake for 25 to 30 minutes.

• • • • • • • • • • • • • • • •

Serve with crackers or potato chips.

Hot Shrimp Dip

2   8-ounce packages cream cheese
1   10-ounce can diced tomatoes
    and green chilies
1   4 1/4-ounce can tiny or small
    shrimp, drained

2   tablespoons diced bell pepper
3   green onions, chopped
1/4 teaspoon Worcestershire sauce

Combine all ingredients in a medium saucepan and cook over medium heat until the cream cheese is completely melted. Sever with tortilla chips or crackers. Refrigerate leftovers and re-heat later in microwave.

Appetizers

Jalapeño Corn Cheese Dip

2	16-ounce cans sweet corn	1	10-ounce package grated sharp Cheddar cheese
1	4-ounce can chopped green chilies	1	cup mayonnaise
5	green onions, chopped	1	cup sour cream
½	cup chopped jalapeño peppers	¼	teaspoon garlic powder
1	10-ounce package grated Monterey Jack cheese		

Stir and chill. Serve with corn chips. This makes a large portion.

Lemon Rotel Mold

1	can diced Rotel tomatoes	¼	cup chopped green onion
¼	cup milk	½	cup chopped celery
1	3-ounce package lemon gelatin	½	cup chopped pecans
1	8-ounce package cream cheese, softened	½	cup Miracle Whip, do not substitute
½	cup chopped green pepper		

Combine tomatoes, milk, gelatin and cream cheese in saucepan. Heat and stir until melted. Fold in remaining ingredients. Pour into mold that has been lined with plastic wrap. Chill overnight. Serve with buttery crackers.

Appetizers

Mexican Cheesecake

2   8-ounce packages cream cheese
2   cups shredded Monterey Jack
      cheese
1   24-ounce carton sour cream
3   eggs
1   cup salsa

1   4-ounce can diced green chili
      peppers, drained
1   cup guacamole
1   tomato, chopped
      Tortilla chips

Preheat oven to 350°. Beat cream cheese and Monterey Jack cheese until fluffy. Beat in 8-ounces sour cream and add the eggs all at once. Continue to beat at low speed until just combined. Stir in salsa and chili peppers. Pour into a 9-inch springform pan. Set the pan on a baking sheet. Bake for 40 to 45 minutes, or until the center is almost set. Immediately spread the remaining sour cream over the top, being careful, as the top of the cheesecake will be delicate. Cool on a wire rack. Cover and refrigerate for 3 to 24 hours. Remove the cheesecake from the pan and garnish with guacamole in a ring. Top with the chopped tomatoes. Serve with the tortilla chips.

Mexican Layered Dip

1   large can bean dip
1   can chopped green chilies
1   pint sour cream
1   package taco seasoning
1   small can chopped olives
1   large tomato, diced

1   jar salsa
5   green onions, chopped
1   pint guacamole dip
1   jar bacon bits
2   cups shredded Cheddar cheese

Add taco seasoning to sour cream, blend well. Layer ingredients in the order they are listed above in an 8x8-inch dish. Let set overnight in the refrigerator.

Appetizers

Olive and Cream Cheese Sandwich Spread

1   8-ounce package cream cheese, softened
1   jar green olives

mayonnaise
salt and pepper, to taste
chopped boiled eggs, optional

Whip cream cheese adding mayonnaise to make it creamier. Add olives and eggs then refrigerate. Use party ryes or white bread cut into small rounds.

Olive Dip

1   can black olives, chopped
1   tomato, chopped
1   bunch green onions
1   large bag shredded cheese
    (4 cheese or Monterey Jack)

½   cup Italian dressing
1   can green chilies, chopped
2   tablespoons chopped cilantro

Mix together and serve with corn chips.

Onion Dip

3   sweet (or white) onions, cut in chunks

2   cups shredded Swiss cheese
1   cup mayonnaise

Mix together and put in a 9x13-inch dish and bake at 350° for 45 minutes or until it starts to brown. Serve with tortilla chips.

Appetizers

Open Face Shrimp Sandwiches

2   teaspoons butter, melted
     thyme
1   4-ounce can baby shrimp (can
     use chopped fresh shrimp)
½   cup mozzarella cheese

½   cup mayonnaise
½   cup fresh bread crumbs
¼   teaspoon garlic salt
     white bread cut into rounds

Brush bread with melted butter and sprinkle heavy with thyme, toast in oven for 5 minutes, can be done the night before. Mix the rest of the ingredients the night before. Spread on bread the day of and put in oven on 350° for 15 minutes.

Parmesan Bacon Sticks

15   center cut bacon slices, cut in
     half lengthwise
1   3-ounce package of thin bread
     sticks (30 in a box)

½   cup fresh or can Parmesan
     cheese

Wrap bacon strips around bread and roll in cheese. Place on baking sheet, close together. Bake at 250° for 1 hour (or longer) until bacon is crisp.

2½ DOZEN.

Pecan Christmas Cheese Ball

2   8-ounce packages cream cheese
1   jar dried beef
3   green onions

1   small jar chopped black olives
2   teaspoons garlic powder
¾   cup pecan pieces

Combine cream cheese, dried beef, green onions, black olives and garlic powder. Mix well. Form a large ball. Roll cheese ball in pecan pieces. Serve with crackers.

Appetizers

Pecan Olive Roll

1½ cups flour
¾ teaspoon salt
½ teaspoon paprika
½ cup butter
½ cup sour cream
¾ cup chopped pecans

¾ cup grated sharp Cheddar
   cheese
¾ cup chopped pimento-stuffed
   green olives
½ tablespoon mayonnaise

Sift flour with salt and paprika into mixing bowl. Cut in butter. Add sour cream and mix well. Cover and chill dough ½ hour. Mix pecans, cheese, olives, and mayonnaise. Divide dough into 2 balls. Roll each into an 8x11-inch rectangle, then cut into two 4-inch wide strips. Spread olive filling down the center of each strip. Bring long sides together and pinch to seal. Pinch ends together. Place on a baking sheet, seam side down. Bake in 400° oven for 20 minutes or until brown and crisp. Cool and slice.

3 DOZEN SLICES.

"Philly" Bacon Wreath

2 8-ounce packages cream cheese,
   softened
½ cup Miracle Whip
⅓ cup Parmesan cheese

10 slices bacon, fried crisp and
   crumbled
½ cup chopped green onion
½ cup chopped fine bell pepper
   small jar pimento diced, optional

Mix together. Form wreath. Decorate with strips of pimento and fresh parsley.

When serving, surround with assorted crackers.

May also be used as a spread.

Pepperoni Herb Cheese Cake

Crust

1	cup all-purpose flour
½	cup salted butter, chilled

1	large egg yolk
2	teaspoons grated lemon zest

Filling

2 cloves garlic

1 large onion

⅔ cup chopped fresh parsley

¾ cup freshly grated Parmesan cheese

3 8-ounce packages cream cheese, room temperature

3 tablespoons all-purpose flour

4 large eggs

2 teaspoons salt

½ teaspoon hot sauce

2 tablespoons fresh lemon juice

1 tablespoon fresh oregano, chopped (or 1 teaspoon dried)

1 tablespoon fresh tarragon, chopped (or 1 teaspoon dried)

1 tablespoon fresh basil, chopped (or 1 teaspoon dried)

½ tablespoon fresh rosemary, chopped (or ½ teaspoon dried)

½ cup chopped pepperoni
fresh herbs for garnish
crackers for serving

For the crust, in a food processor, blend flour, butter, egg yolk, and lemon zest to a cornmeal-like consistency. Remove dough from bowl and knead lightly. Shape into ball, wrap in waxed paper, and refrigerate until slightly chilled. Evenly press ⅓ of dough into bottom of 8-inch springform pan and press remaining dough around sides. Store in freezer while preparing filling. Chop garlic in processor; add onion, then parsley and Parmesan cheese. Add cream cheese, one package at a time, and process. Add flour and 1 egg and continue processing until smooth. Add remaining 3 eggs, one at a time, blending well after each addition. Add salt, hot sauce, lemon juice, and herbs, processing just until blended. Stir in pepperoni and pour into dough-lined pan. Bake at 400° for 10 minutes, reduce temperature to 325°, and bake 1 hour longer or until done. Let stand 1 hour before serving. Garnish with fresh herbs and serve with your choice of crackers.

Appetizers

Pickled Party Shrimp

5 pounds large fresh shrimp	½ cup pickling spices
tops from ½ bunch celery	Boiling water
	3½ teaspoons salt

Sauce

2½ cups olive oil	3 tablespoons salt
5 tablespoons capers and juice	1½ cups white vinegar
5 teaspoons celery seeds	dash of Tabasco sauce
2 large onions, sliced	

Take 5 pounds large fresh shrimp add enough boiling water to cover. Add celery tops salt and pickling spices. Cook shrimp until shell begins to separate from meat. Drain, peel, and devein. Alternate layers of cleaned shrimp and thinly sliced onions in shallow dish. Add 7 or 8 bay leaves. Mix sauce well and pour over shrimp and onions. Cover and store in refrigerator for 24 hours.

Pineapple Salsa

½ small pineapple, cored for wedges, chopped, and juices reserved	1 small jalapeño pepper (ribs and seeds removed for less heat, if desired), minced
	2 teaspoons chopped cilantro
	salt and pepper

In a medium bowl, toss together all ingredients. Serve as a side dish. It is good with grilled fish.

Pizza Dip

1   8-ounce package cream cheese
1   10-ounce jar pizza sauce
1   4¼-ounce can chopped black olives
⅓   cup chopped purple onion
1   package pepperoni cut into quarters
1½ cups grated mozzarella cheese

Preheat oven to 350°. Place cream cheese in a 9½-inch round dish. Spread throughout bottom layer of the pan. Layer the ingredients in order listed. Bake for 20 minutes. Serve with corn chips.

Pumpkin Bread Sandwiches

3½ cups sifted flour
2   teaspoons baking soda
1½ teaspoons salt
2   teaspoons cinnamon
2   teaspoons nutmeg
3   cups sugar
4   eggs, beaten
⅔   cup water
1   cup salad oil
1   16-ounce can pumpkin
1   cup chopped pecans

Combine flour, baking soda, salt, cinnamon, nutmeg, and sugar in large mixing bowl. Add eggs, water, oil, and pumpkin: stir until blended. Add nuts: mix well. Pour mixture into 3 greased and floured 1 pound coffee cans (12 or 13-ounce will work fine). Bake 1 hour at 350°. Cool slightly in cans: turn out on rack to finish cooling. Flavor is best if baked day before using.

Filling
3   8-ounce packages cream cheese cheesecake flavor

Slice bread. Spread with filling. Cut slices into fourths.

• • • • • • • • • • • • • • •

Keeps for weeks in refrigerator or freezes beautifully. Delicious with spiced tea.

Appetizers

Sausage Roll

2	rolls sausage, hot or regular	2	cloves crushed garlic
2	eggs		seasoning salt and pepper,
1	medium onion, chopped fine		to taste
1	roll buttery crackers, crushed fine		

Mix all ingredients well in a bowl. Spray a Bundt pan really well and evenly place sausage mixture in pan. Cook at 350° for about 30 to 45 minutes until golden brown. Will need to be drained intermittently. Turn out on oven safe plate and put back in oven a few minutes until browned to satisfaction. Slice and serve with buttery crackers.

Men love this!!

Shrimp Dip

1	5-ounce can shrimp	1	8-ounce package cream cheese, softened
2	teaspoons lemon juice		
3	tablespoons mayonnaise		pepper, to taste
1	tablespoon ketchup		Worcestershire sauce, to taste
¼	teaspoon relish		

Drain shrimp. Mince shrimp in bowl with a fork. Add lemon juice. Let sit for 10 minutes. Add cream cheese, mayonnaise, ketchup, relish, pepper and Worcestershire sauce. Serve with crackers.

Shrimp Tea Sandwiches

1   3-ounce package cream cheese,
      softened
2   tablespoons mayonnaise

1   can tiny shrimp
1   teaspoon lemon juice
2   teaspoons grated fresh parsley

Mash shrimp with fork and add lemon juice. Mix cream cheese with mayonnaise and parsley. Add shrimp and lemon juice. Spread on bread cut with cookie cutters.

Shrimp Spread

5   pounds peeled shrimp boiled in
      crab boil seasoning
4   medium onions
1   bunch celery hearts and leaves
1   bunch fresh parsley, to taste

1   quart + 1 cup mayonnaise
1   clove garlic, to taste
    salt and coarse ground pepper,
      to taste
1/2 lemon squeezed (juice)

Put all ingredients through a meat grinder and mix together. Refrigerate over night. Serve with crackers.

Smoked Salmon Spread

1   15 1/2-ounce can salmon
1   teaspoon lemon juice
2   teaspoons horseradish
2   teaspoons grated onion
1/2 cup chopped pecans

1/4 teaspoon liquid smoke
1   8-ounce package cream cheese,
      softened
    salt and pepper, to taste

Mix all ingredients well. Put in fish mold or shape into a log. Chill well and serve with crackers or party breads.

South of the Border Dip

1	pound ground chuck
1	cup cooked rice
1	package taco seasoning
1	can tomato soup
1	large can whole kernel corn, drained
1¼	pounds processed cheese, cubed
1	can Rotel, diced tomatoes and chilies

Brown ground chuck in skillet or microwave. Stir in taco seasoning. Add all other ingredients and heat until cheese is melted. Serve with tortilla chips or dip style corn chips.

Spinach Tarts

1	10-ounce package frozen chopped spinach, thawed and drained
2	eggs, beaten
1	cup grated Romano cheese
2	tablespoons chopped onion
¼	teaspoon salt
¼	teaspoon pepper
¼	nutmeg
24	tart shells

Preheat oven to 375°. Squeeze spinach between paper towels to remove excess moisture. In medium bowl, combine beaten eggs, Romano cheese, onion, salt pepper, and nutmeg. Place spinach in tart shells and pour egg mixture over spinach. Bake for 30 to 35 minutes or until filling is set.

Spinach Crêpes

1	9-ounce package frozen spinach	1½	cups Ricotta cheese
⅔	cup gourmet spreadable garlic and herb cheese or garlic and herb cream cheese	¼	teaspoon ground sage
		¼	cup finely chopped pistachios flour tortillas

Cook, drain and squeeze dry spinach in paper towels. Mix all ingredients together. Spread thinly on to flour tortillas and roll into log shape. Refrigerate 3 to 4 hours before slicing.

Strawberry Party Sandwiches

3	ounces cream cheese	2	tablespoons mashed strawberries and juice
5	strawberries	1	tablespoon confectioners' sugar

Mix together and spread on flattened bread cut in shapes with cookie cutter.

Stuffed French Bread Appetizers

1	loaf French bread	4	ounces sour cream
1	8-ounce package cream cheese	1	small can green chilies, chopped
1	1-ounce package sharp Cheddar cheese	1	roll hot sausage, cooked and drained

Mix all ingredients together well. Cut off top of bread and pack inside of bread. Cover with aluminum foil and bake for 1 to 1½ hours in a 350° oven. Serve with corn chips.

Appetizers

Stuffed Mushrooms

2	dozen mushrooms		1	4¼-ounce can crabmeat
1	stick butter		½	teaspoon salt
1	white onion		½	cup Italian bread crumbs
1	celery stalk			dash of black or red pepper
1	garlic clove			Parmesan cheese
1	tablespoon dried parsley flakes			

Wash mushrooms, remove and reserve stems. Finely mince onion, celery, garlic and mushroom stems. Melt butter in skillet and sauté onion, celery, garlic and mushrooms stems until soft. Add parsley flakes, salt, crabmeat and bread crumbs. Stir until blended completely. Stuff mushroom caps, sprinkle with Parmesan cheese and place in casserole dish. Bake in oven at 350° for 25 to 30 minutes. Serve hot.

Sun-Dried Tomato and Feta Cheese Ball

½	cup unsalted butter, softened		2½	cloves garlic, minced
1	8-ounce package cream cheese, softened		1	tablespoon Greek seasoning
1	4-ounce package feta cheese, crumbled and room temperature		1	teaspoon dried basil
			½	teaspoon red pepper
½	cup chopped green onions			chopped fresh parsley, for garnish
½	cup sun-dried tomatoes, finely chopped			crackers

Blend all ingredients except garnish until well combined. Chill about 2 hours. Shape into a ball and roll in chopped parsley. Serve with crackers.

Appetizers

Sweet and Sour Meatballs

2	pounds ground hamburger meat	1/2	teaspoon garlic powder
1	cup crushed corn flakes	2	eggs
2	tablespoons soy sauce		black pepper, to taste

Sauce

1	can cranberry sauce	2	tablespoons brown sugar
1	12-ounce jar chili sauce		

Mix all ingredients together and form into small balls. Pour sauce over balls and bake 1 hour at 350°.

Taco Roll-Ups

2	8-ounce packages cream cheese, softened	2	cups finely shredded Cheddar cheese
1	4½-ounce can chopped ripe olives, drained	1	tablespoon onion soup mix
1	cup sour cream	1/2	cup picante sauce
2	tablespoons taco seasoning	8	10-inch flour tortillas

In a small mixing bowl, beat cream cheese and sour cream until smooth; stir in the Cheddar cheese, picante sauce, olives, taco seasoning and soup mix. Spread over tortillas; roll up jelly-roll style. Wrap in plastic wrap and refrigerate for at least 1 hour. Just before serving, cut into 1-inch pieces.

APPROXIMATELY 3½ DOZEN.

Appetizers

Tailgate Sandwiches

Hawaiian rolls
1 pound shredded ham
1/3 cup Swiss cheese
1/2 teaspoon margarine

1 teaspoon Worcestershire sauce
3 tablespoons poppy seeds
3 tablespoons mustard
1/2 medium onion, grated

Split rolls and put ham and cheese on one side. Mix margarine, Worcestershire sauce, poppy seeds, mustard and onions. Place the spreading mixture on one side of the rolls. Wrap in foil and bake 15 minutes at 400°.

Tennessee Caviar

1 15.8-ounce can black-eyed peas
1 15-ounce can corn
1-2 Roma tomatoes
4 green onions
1/2 red bell pepper, chopped

1 cup picante sauce
1/4 cup fresh cilantro
2 cloves garlic, minced
2 tablespoons lime juice
tortilla chips

Rinse and drain peas and corn. Stir together peas, corn, tomatoes and next 5 ingredients in a serving bowl. Cover and chill at least 2 hours. Even better if made a day ahead. Serve with tortilla chips.

Tomato and Basil Salsa

1/2 cup chopped fresh basil
2 garlic cloves, minced
1/4 teaspoon salt
freshly ground pepper, to taste

1/4 cup balsamic vinegar
1 tablespoon extra virgin olive oil
1 pound ripe tomatoes, cored and chopped

In a bowl, mash basil, garlic, salt, and pepper. Stir in vinegar and oil. Add tomatoes, toss until well combined.

Appetizers

Tomatillo Guacamole

10	tomatillos (remove husks) cut into quarters	1	lime
1	tablespoon cilantro	1	medium onion, cut into quarters
2	avocados, peeled and cut into quarters	1	teaspoon salt
		2	jalapeño peppers

Place first 4 ingredients into food processor. Add salt, cilantro and lime juice from lime. Add jalapeño peppers to heat things up.

Tomato Cups

1	8-ounce package shredded Cheddar cheese	3/4	cup mayonnaise
1	8-ounce can bacon bits	1	can Rotel tomatoes, original
		2½	cans flaky biscuits

Mix the first 4 ingredients together. Press each flake from 1 biscuit into a muffin pan. Scoop the mixture into the muffin pan on top of the biscuit flake. Do not over fill the cups or they will spill over during cooking. Bake at 400° for 9 minutes.

Tortilla Roll-Ups

1	pound cream cheese	1	4-ounce jar green chilies
1	package powdered Italian dressing	1	small can chopped black olives, drained
3	green onions, chopped	4	12-inch tortillas
1	4-ounce jar pimentos, drained	10	10-inch tortillas

Mix all ingredients. Spread on tortilla, roll tortilla as firmly as possible. Wrap each roll in wax paper. Refrigerate for at least 2 hours. Cut off ends and cut slices ¾-inch thick.

Appetizers

Two-Day Swiss Spread

1 12-ounce package shredded Swiss cheese	1 teaspoon seasoned salt
1/2-1 cup mayonnaise	1 teaspoon dry mustard
2 large green peppers, chopped	4 dashes hot sauce

Chop peppers and cheese. Mix with rest of ingredients and refrigerate 24 to 48 hours before serving. Aging improves taste. Serve with Wheat Thins.

Veggie Party Sandwiches

2/3 cup carrots, peeled and grated	1/4 cup celery, chopped
1/2 tablespoon mayonnaise	1/4 teaspoon salt
1/2 cup onions, minced	2 tablespoons lemon juice
1/4 cup green pepper, minced	1 8-ounce package cream cheese, softened
1/4 cup cucumber, peeled and chopped	

Mix all together well. Spread onto party ryes or other bread cut into rounds.

Vidalia Onion Cheese Dip

3 large sweet onions, coarsely chopped	2 cups shredded sharp Cheddar cheese
2 tablespoons unsalted butter or margarine, melted	1 cup mayonnaise
	1/2 teaspoon hot sauce
	1 garlic clove, minced

Cook onion in butter in a large skillet over medium-high heat, stirring constantly, until tender. Combine onion, cheese, mayonnaise, hot sauce, and garlic; stir well. Pour into a lightly buttered 1½-quart casserole. Bake, uncovered, at 375° for 20 to 25 minutes or until bubbly and golden. Serve dip with tortilla chips or assorted crackers.

Appetizers

Notes

Notes

_____

_____

_____

_____

_____

_____

_____

_____

_____

_____

_____

_____

_____

_____

_____

_____

Beverages

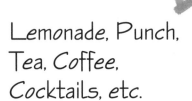

Lemonade, Punch,
Tea, Coffee,
Cocktails, etc.

Back Bay Lemonade

1	12-ounce can limeade, thawed	1	12-ounce can Mexican light beer
1	12-ounce can lemon-lime soda		12-ounce tequila

Slowly stir all ingredients together; otherwise, it will foam over.

Refrigerate and serve over ice. This can be refrigerated for up to 3 days as long as it is in a covered container. This is a refreshing drink for a hot summer day.

Blush Punch

1	750-ml bottle champagne, chilled	1	12-ounce can frozen lemonade concentrate
1	750-ml bottle white Zinfandel, chilled	1	64-ounce bottle cranberry juice cocktail
		1-2	cups lemon-lime soda, to taste

Mix champagne, Zinfandel, lemonade concentrate, cranberry juice cocktail, and lemon-lime soda together. Pour into champagne flute and serve immediately.

Citrus Mimosa

1	cup frozen strawberry daiquiri mix	3/4	cup water
		1/3	cup grapefruit juice
1	6-ounce can frozen orange juice concentrate	1	3-ounce can frozen limeade concentrate

Mix daiquiri mix, orange juice concentrate, water, grapefruit juice and limeade concentrate and refrigerate. Mix equal parts with chilled champagne; garnish with ½ orange slice. Pour into champagne flute and serve immediately.

Beverages

Banana Slush Punch

6	cups water	1	12-ounce can frozen lemonade
1	46-ounce can pineapple juice	2	64-ounce bottles ginger ale
4	cups sugar	1	12-ounce can frozen orange juice
5	bananas, mashed		

Combine sugar and water. Bring to a boil stirring until sugar dissolves. Let cool. Add mashed bananas to the sugar mixture. Prepare the lemonade and orange juice according to the directions on the can. Add pineapple, lemonade and orange juices to the sugar mixture. Freeze. When ready to be used, set frozen mixture out for 2 hours. Pour ginger ale over the mixture. It should be slushy.

50 SERVINGS.

Blackberry Iced Tea

3	cups fresh or frozen blackberries, thawed	4	cups boiling water
1¼	cups sugar	2	family-size tea bags
1	tablespoon chopped fresh mint	2½	cups cold water
¼	teaspoon baking soda		garnishes: fresh blackberries, fresh mint sprigs

Combine blackberries and sugar in large container. Crush blackberries with wooden spoon. Add mint and baking soda. Set aside. Pour 4 cups boiling water over tea bags; cover and let stand 3 minutes. Discard tea bags. Pour tea over blackberry mixture; let stand at room temperature 1 hour. Pour tea through a wire-mesh strainer into a large pitcher, discarding solids. Add 2½ cups cold water, stirring until sugar dissolves. Cover and chill until ready to serve. Garnish, if desired.

Coconut Coffee

2   cups half-and-half
4   cups freshly brewed coffee

1   15-ounce can cream of coconut
    sweetened whipped cream

Bring half-and-half and cream of coconut to a boil in a large saucepan over medium heat, stirring constantly. Stir in brewed coffee and garnish with sweetened whipped cream.

8 CUPS.

Coffee Punch

1   gallon strong cold coffee
4   cups cold milk
1   cup sugar
4   teaspoons vanilla

2   quarts vanilla ice cream
2   cups whipped cream
    garnish with nutmeg

Combine coffee, cold milk, sugar and vanilla together until sugar dissolves. Pour over ice cream and top with whipped cream. Sprinkle with nutmeg.

Champagne Punch

6   cups cranberry juice cocktail,
    chilled
2   cups orange juice, chilled

2   750-ml bottles champagne,
    chilled
1   64-ounce bottle club soda,
    chilled

Mix cranberry juice cocktail, orange juice, champagne and club soda together. Pour into champagne flutes and serve immediately.

Beverages

Easy Cranberry Ice

2   cups water
1   cup sugar

2½ cups cranberry juice cocktail

Combine water and sugar in a saucepan. Bring to a boil, stirring until sugar dissolves. Remove from heat. Cool. Stir in cranberry juice. Pour mixture into pan. Cover and freeze until frozen. Remove from freezer; let stand 10 minutes. Shave ice by scraping with a fork. Scoop ice into glasses, and serve immediately or store in a airtight container in freezer until ready to serve.

7 SERVINGS.

Frozen Punch Slush

1   6-ounce can frozen lemonade,
      thawed and diluted
1   12-ounce can frozen orange juice,
      thawed and diluted
1   46-ounce can pineapple juice
3   cups water

3   cups sugar
2   64-ounce bottles of lemon-lime
      carbonated beverage
6   ripe bananas
1   large orange, sliced
1   large lemon, sliced

Combine bananas, lemonade and orange juice in electric blender until smooth. Add pineapple juice, water and sugar to the banana mixture and freeze in a large container. To serve, thaw until slushy, add carbonated beverage, orange and lemon slices and serve in your punch bowl.

35 TO 40 SERVINGS.

● ● ● ● ● ● ● ● ● ● ● ● ● ● ●

Note: This will keep in the refrigerator for up to ten days. You may refreeze after you remove the fruit slices.

Beverages

Funky Monkey

4	scoops vanilla ice cream
1/2	banana, mashed
1	jigger vodka
1	jigger rum
1	jigger Frangelico
	nutmeg

Blend vanilla ice cream, banana, vodka, rum and Frangelico together. Pour in glass and sprinkle nutmeg on top.

Harvest Punch

3/4	cup sugar
2	cups orange juice
3/4	cup water
1	cup lemon juice
2²/3	cups grape juice

Combine sugar and water in saucepan. Bring to boil, stirring occasionally. Cook over low heat about 5 minutes. Add the grape, lemon and orange juices. Chill well. Pour over ice in a punch bowl.

10 TO 12 SERVINGS.

Jugo Fiojo

1	750-ml bottle champagne, chilled
1/3	cup peach schnapps, chilled
3	cups cranberry juice, chilled
	fresh raspberries to garnish

Mix all ingredients in a pitcher. Serve in champagne flutes and garnish with raspberries.

Beverages

Hot Buttered Rum

1	pound butter	1	teaspoon allspice
1	pound confectioners' sugar	1	quart vanilla ice cream
1	pound light brown sugar	1	jigger rum
1	teaspoon cinnamon	1	jigger brandy
1	teaspoon nutmeg		boiling water

Mix butter, confectioners' sugar, brown sugar, cinnamon, nutmeg, allspice and vanilla ice cream in a saucepan and heat until the ingredients reach the consistency of cake batter. Mixture may be frozen if needed. Mix 1 to 2 tablespoon of the mixture with 1 jigger of rum and 1 jigger of brandy and enough boiling water to fill a mug. Stir to mix.

Hot Chocolate

1/4	cup unsweetened cocoa	3	cups whole milk
1/2	cup sugar	1	cup whipping cream
1 1/4	teaspoons salt	1	teaspoon vanilla extract
1/3	cup hot water		garnish with marshmallows

In a medium saucepan, combine cocoa, sugar and salt. Add hot water, stirring until smooth. Gradually add milk and whipping cream. Heat over medium heat until steaming, but do not boil. Remove from heat and add vanilla. With a wire whisk, beat until frothy. Garnish each serving with marshmallows. Serve immediately.

6 SERVINGS.

Mississippi Punch

1	large box lime gelatin	1	medium bottle lemon juice
1	large can pineapple juice	2½	cups cold water
2	cups boiling water	1	ounce almond extract

Combine gelatin and boiling water; stir well. Add sugar, cold water, pineapple juice, lemon juice and almond extract. Chill 3 to 4 hours before serving.

1 GALLON.

Mr. Funk of New Orleans

1	750-ml bottle champagne, chilled	½ cup peach Schnapps
2½	cups cranberry juice cocktail, chilled	garnish with fresh cranberries

Mix champagne, cranberry juice cocktail and peach Schnapps together. Serve in champagne flutes and garnish.

6 TO 8 SERVINGS.

Orange Julius

1½	cups orange juice	1½	cups milk
½	cup water	¼	cup sugar
½	teaspoon vanilla	10	ice cubes

Mix orange juice, water, vanilla, milk, sugar and ice cubes in a blender on high until well blended. Pour into glasses and serve immediately.

Beverages

Party Punch

1 6-ounce can frozen orange juice concentrate
1 cup water
1 cup milk

¼ cup sugar
1 teaspoon vanilla
ice cubes

Place orange juice concentrate, water, milk, sugar and vanilla together in a blender with 6 to 8 ice cubes. Blend well. Serve immediately.

4 TO 6 SERVINGS.

Peach Punch

4 cups boiling water
3 family-size boxes peach gelatin
4 cups sugar
8 ounce container lemon juice

2 32-ounce cans pineapple juice, unsweetened
9 cups cold water
1 64-ounce bottle ginger ale

Mix boiling water, peach gelatin and sugar together. Stir until the mixture is dissolved. Add lemon juice, pineapple juice and cold water. Freeze. To serve, partially thaw and pour a 64-ounce bottle ginger ale over mixture.

Poinsettia Punch

2 750-ml bottles champagne, chilled
1 quart cranberry juice, chilled

1 cup vodka, optional
garnish with fresh cranberries

Combine champagne, cranberry juice and, if desired, vodka. Serve over crushed ice and garnish with fresh cranberries.

14 SERVINGS.

Beverages

Ruby Champagne Cocktail

2	tablespoons cranberry juice	1	teaspoon grenadine
1	tablespoon orange liqueur	½	cup dry champagne

Combine cranberry juice, orange liqueur and grenadine in a champagne flute. Top-off with champagne.

1 SERVING.

Santa's Last Stop Milk Punch

2	750-ml bottles brandy	1	gallon whole milk
2	cans condensed milk	½	cup confectioners' sugar
2	pints half-and-half	4	tablespoons vanilla

Mix brandy, condensed milk, half-and-half, whole milk, confectioners' sugar and vanilla together and freeze in plastic container.

● ● ● ● ● ● ● ● ● ● ● ● ● ●

Best served when it is slushy.

Smoothies

1	cup fat-free milk	1	medium banana, coarsely chopped
1	pint low-fat frozen vanilla yogurt, softened	½	cup your favorite fresh fruit

Process milk, yogurt, banana and fresh fruit together in a blender until smooth, stopping to scrape down sides. Serve immediately.

Beverages

Spiced Mulled Cider

8 cups apple cider	6 whole cloves
3/4 cup lemon juice	3 cinnamon sticks
1 cup brown sugar	

In a large saucepan, combine apple cider, lemon juice, brown sugar, cloves, and cinnamon sticks. Bring to a boil, reduce heat and simmer for 20 minutes. Remove spices and serve immediately.

2 QUARTS.

Strawberry Tea Slush

2 cups boiling water	1 6-ounce can frozen lemonade concentrate
4 regular-size tea bags	
1½ cups frozen strawberries	1 cup ice cubes
	¼ cup confectioners' sugar

Pour 2 cups of boiling water over tea bags. Cover and steep 5 minutes. Remove tea bags. Chill at least 1 hour. Process chilled tea, frozen strawberries, and remaining ingredients in a blender until smooth and slushy. Serve immediately.

Swiss Kiss Martini

1 chilled martini glass decorated with chocolate syrup swirls	½ ounce Frangelico
	1 ounce dark crème de cocoa
2 ounces vodka	1 tablespoon half-and-half
½ ounce butterscotch schnapps	

Fill shaker with ice. Combine vodka, schnapps, Frangelico, crème de cocoa and half-and-half. Shake well. Strain into martini glass and serve.

Beverages

Spiced Tea

6   small tea bags
2   teaspoon whole cloves
2   sticks cinnamon
1   quart boiling water
2   cups sugar

2   cups pineapple juice
1   6-ounce can frozen orange juice,
     undiluted
3/4 cup lemon juice

Combine boiling water, tea bags, cloves, and cinnamon sticks. Steep for
15 minutes. Add sugar, pineapple juice, frozen orange juice and lemon juice.
Heat and serve.

● ● ● ● ● ● ● ● ● ● ● ● ● ● ●

Stores in the refrigerator or may be frozen.

Strawberry Champagne Punch

1   3-ounce box strawberry-flavor
     gelatin
1   cup boiling water
1   6-ounce can frozen lemonade
     concentrate
2   cups cold water

1   750-ml bottle rosé wine, chilled
1   750-ml bottle champagne,
     chilled
1   pint fresh strawberries with
     stems

Dissolve gelatin in boiling water and set aside to cool. In punch bowl, combine
gelatin mixture, thawed lemonade concentrate and cold water. Just before
serving, stir in wine, champagne and strawberries.

● ● ● ● ● ● ● ● ● ● ● ● ● ●

*To freeze strawberries, wash and gently dry. If desired, leave stems on to add
color. Arrange on a cookie sheet in a single layer; freeze until firm.*

Beverages

Tequila Sour Slushy

1	pint orange juice	1	pint tequila
1	pint lemonade		

Mix the orange juice, lemonade and tequila together and place in freezer. When ready to serve, put mixture in a glass with a spoon.

Vodka Slush

2	64-ounce bottles lemon-lime soda	1	6-ounce can orange juice
1	48-ounce can pineapple juice	2	ounces water
1	cup water	1	10-ounce jar cherries with juice
1	cup sugar	1	750-ml bottle Vodka

Mix lemon line soda, pineapple juice, water and sugar together in large plastic container. Place orange juice, water and jar of cherries in blender and blend well. Pour into large container with first ingredients and add vodka. Mix well and freeze. Remove from freezer 1 hour prior to serving.

Whispers

1	quart coffee ice cream, slightly softened	¼	cup cognac
¼	cup crème de cacao	¼	cup coffee-flavored liqueur

Process ice cream, crème de cacao, cognac and coffee- flavored liqueur in blender until smooth. Pour mixture into chilled stemmed glasses; serve immediately.

3 CUPS.

Beverages

Wassail

2 quarts cranberry juice
2²/₃ quarts apple juice
1 pint pineapple juice
²/₃ cup brown sugar

²/₃ teaspoon salt
5¹/₃ sticks cinnamon
2 teaspoons whole cloves
2 tablespoons red hots

Use a percolator coffee pot to make this wassail. In the top basket part of the pot, add the sugar, salt, cinnamon, cloves, and red hots. In the bottom portion of the pot, add cranberry, apple and pineapple juices. Turn the percolator on and heat until ready to serve.

White Chocolate Latte

2 cups milk
1 cup half-and-half
²/₃ cup white chocolate morsels
2 tablespoons instant coffee
   granules

1 teaspoon vanilla extract
¹/₄ teaspoon almond extract
   whipped cream, optional
   garnish with cinnamon sticks

Stir milk, half-and-half, white chocolate morsels and instant coffee granules together in a small saucepan over low heat until white chocolate morsels are melted. Stir in vanilla and almond extracts; pour evenly into 4 mugs. Top with whipped cream, if desired. Garnish, if desired, and serve immediately.

Watermelon-Cranberry Mint Mixer

¼ whole watermelon
1 quart cranberry juice

¼ cup fresh mint leaves, julienned

Remove seeds from the watermelon, place in blender, pour in cranberry juice and mint leaves. Blend until watermelon is pulpy. Set it aside for a few hours to infuse mint flavor. Pour over ice and serve.

• • • • • • • • • • • • • • • •

Add a splash of vodka, if desired.

Winter Holiday Apéritif

⅓ cup champagne
⅓ cup cranberry juice

1 tablespoon orange liqueur

Pour champagne into glass; add cranberry juice and orange liqueur.

1 SERVING.

Won't Send You Into a Sugar-Coma Punch

1 64-ounce bottle Sprite, chilled
1 64-ounce bottle white grape
  juice, chilled

cherries, cranberries, grapes, orange slices, strawberries, optional

Mix 1 bottle of Sprite (can use other lemon-lime sodas, but it may make it sweeter) with 1 bottle of white grape juice. Add fruit of your choice and serve immediately.

2 GALLONS.

Beverages

Notes

Salads & Soups

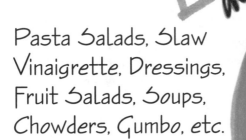

Pasta Salads, Slaw
Vinaigrette, Dressings,
Fruit Salads, Soups,
Chowders, Gumbo, etc.

Almond Strawberry Salad

3   cups fresh baby spinach
1   tablespoon cider vinegar
½   cup sliced fresh strawberries
1   tablespoon honey

¼   cup sliced honey-roasted almonds
1½   teaspoons sugar

In a large bowl, combine spinach, strawberries and almonds. In a jar with a tight-fitting lid, combine vinegar, honey and sugar; shake well. Drizzle over salad and toss to coat. Serve immediately.

4 SERVINGS.

Apple Cashew Salad

2   5-ounce pieces Romaine lettuce
1   cup shredded Swiss cheese
1   cup cashews

1   apple, coarsely chopped
1   pear, coarsely chopped
¼   cup sweetened, dried cranberries

Salad Dressing

½   cup sugar
⅓   cup lemon juice
2   teaspoon red onion, finely chopped

1   teaspoon salt
⅔   cup oil
1   tablespoon poppy seeds

Combine all ingredients in a large serving bowl; toss to mix. Pour salad dressing over salad and toss.

8 TO 10 SERVINGS.

Baked Chicken Salad

2   cups cubed baked chicken, cooled
½   cup chopped bell pepper
2   cups chopped celery
½   cup Miracle Whip
½   cup chopped toasted almonds
2   tablespoons chopped pimento

½   teaspoon salt
2   tablespoons lemon juice
2   tablespoons grated onion
½   cup grated Cheddar cheese
    crushed potato chips

Combine all ingredients except cheese and chips. Toss lightly then spoon into 1½-quart casserole dish. Spread cheese and chips on top. Bake at 350° for 25 minutes or until bubbly and hot.

Balsamic Vinaigrette

1   tablespoon red wine vinegar
    (try thyme, rosemary or basil
    flavored vinegars)
1½ tablespoons Balsamic vinegar
1   tablespoon Dijon mustard
½   teaspoon salt

1   garlic clove, crushed
    black pepper
¾   cup good quality olive oil
1   teaspoon sugar or brown sugar,
    optional

Mix well the vinegars, mustard, salt, and garlic. Slowly add olive oil, whisking well. Add freshly ground black pepper, to taste. Add more Balsamic vinegar, to taste if desired.

To achieve a slightly different flavor, add up to 1 teaspoon of sugar or brown sugar.

Black Bean Salad

2	15-ounce cans black beans, drained and rinsed	½	cup chopped celery
1	cup chopped tomatoes	1	tablespoon lemon rind
¾	cup chopped green or red pepper	1	clove garlic minced
⅔	cup sliced green onion	2	tablespoons chopped cilantro

Combine ingredients and set aside while preparing Vinaigrette Dressing.

Vinaigrette Dressing

½	cup olive oil	⅓	cup sliced green onion
¼	cup Balsamic vinegar	1	teaspoon Dijon mustard
¼	teaspoon red pepper		fresh ground pepper
1	tablespoon basil		

Whisk vinegar, mustard, basil and red pepper. Whisk in oil. Stir in onion and pepper. Pour over black bean salad.

● ● ● ● ● ● ● ● ● ● ● ● ● ●

Serve a grilled salmon steak on top of this salad.

Broccoli Salad

2	large heads broccoli	¼	cup raisins
10	slices bacon, crisp and crumbled	¼	red bell pepper (small amount to add color)
1	small onion, chopped		

Dressing

⅔	cup mayonnaise	3	tablespoons sugar
½	tablespoon apple cider vinegar		

Mix all ingredients and let stand in refrigerator overnight

Salads & Soups

Chicken Mandarin Salad

3 cups chopped chicken	1/2 teaspoon salt
1 cups diced celery	1 cup seedless grapes
2 tablespoons lemon juice	(red or green)
1 tablespoon minced onion	1 10-ounce can Mandarin oranges
1/3 cup mayonnaise	croissant rolls

Combine first 4 ingredients cover and chill at least 1 hour. Combine mayonnaise and salt. Add mayonnaise mixture, grapes and walnuts to chilled chicken mixture. Serve on croissant rolls.

Chicken Salad

4 cups cooked and chopped chicken	1/2 teaspoon curry powder
2 cups chopped celery	1 can water chestnuts
1 1/2 cups mayonnaise	1 can slivered almonds
	1 teaspoon salt

Drain water chestnuts, slice and mix with chicken. Mix mayonnaise with curry powder and salt, add to chicken mixture. Add celery and almonds and toss lightly. Refrigerate for several hours. Serve on lettuce.

8 TO 10 SERVINGS.

Chicken Salad

2 pounds chicken, grilled and cut to bite-size
1 package frozen peas, cooked
1 box wild rice
2 cups white rice

1 cup celery
½ cup green onion
1 cup toasted almonds
1 jar French Vinaigrette

Mix all ingredients. Refrigerate overnight.

10 SERVINGS.

Corn Salad

1 can yellow kernel corn
1 can white niblet corn
1 can shoe peg corn
   salt, to taste

   pepper, to taste
2 green onions, chopped
1 tomato, chopped, optional
2 tablespoons mayonnaise

Mix all together, refrigerate and then bring out 10 minutes prior to serving, stir well.

6 TO 8 SERVINGS.

Easy Fruit Salad

2 cups fresh sliced strawberries
3 cups seedless green grapes
3 bananas, sliced

1 8-ounce container strawberry yogurt

Combine strawberries, green grapes and sliced bananas. Add strawberry yogurt and mix until fruit is covered.

Cucumber and Shells Salad

1 16-ounce package medium-size pasta shells
1 16-ounce package frozen green peas, thawed

1 medium cucumber, halved and sliced
1 small red onion, chopped
1 cup ranch salad dressing

Cook pasta according to package directions; drain and rinse in cold water. In a large bowl, combine pasta, peas, cucumber and onion. Add dressing, toss to coat. Cover and chill for at least 2 hours before serving.

12 SERVINGS.

Curried Chicken Salad

6 chicken breasts, bone in, skin on
olive oil
salt
black pepper

1½ cups good mayonnaise
3 tablespoons curry powder
3 stalks celery, diced
2 green onions, chopped

Preheat the oven to 350°. Place the chicken breast on pan and rub the skin with olive oil. Sprinkle liberally with salt and pepper. Roast for 35 to 40 minutes, until the chicken is just cooked. Set aside until cool enough to handle. Once cool remove the meat and dice into bite-sized pieces. Combine the mayonnaise, curry powder, and 1½ teaspoons of salt and process in the food processor until smooth. Combine the chicken with enough dressing to moisten. Add the celery, and green onions, and mix well. Refrigerate for several hours to allow the flavor to blend.

6 SERVINGS.

Fresh Vegetable Chopped Salad

2	cups water		1	large fresh tomato
2	large carrots		1	ripe avocado
2	ears fresh corn		1	heaping tablespoon Dijon mustard
1/3	pound fresh green beans		1/4	cup salad vinegar (or sherry vinegar)
1	small cucumber		1/2	cup extra light olive oil
1	small red onion (about 1/4 cup diced)			salt
1	cup diced Radicchio (purple) lettuce			fresh ground pepper

In a medium pot, boil water with a tablespoon of salt. Peel and dice carrots into small cubes (no bigger than 1/2-inch). Discard the ends off the green beans and chop into similar size pieces. Peel husk from fresh corn. Place corn in boiling water. After 2 minutes, add carrots, after 1 minute add beans. Cook an additional 3 minutes and strain all in a colander. Rinse immediately with cold water to stop the cooking process. Peel and dice cucumber. Dice red onion and chop radicchio lettuce. Cut corn, sliding knife where the kernels meet the cob, from top to base. In a medium-size bowl pour extra light olive oil. Gradually whisk in salad vinegar and Dijon mustard. Salt and pepper, to taste.

Combine all chopped ingredients with vinaigrette. Chill at least 1 hour and up to 2 days. When ready to serve, chop the peeled and seeded tomato, and the avocado into same size pieces, and add to mixture. Toss and serve.

• • • • • • • • • • • • • •

Serve on a platter on top of a bed of lettuce, or in a casserole dish, or plate using a round mold. This dish is excellent for entertaining, as most of it can be made the day before, and it is a colorful, healthy side dish/salad.

Frozen Cranberry Salad

2 3-ounce packages cream cheese, softened	1 8-ounce can crushed pineapple, drained
2 tablespoons mayonnaise	1/2 cup chopped pecans
2 tablespoons sugar	1 teaspoon vanilla
1 16-ounce can whole berry cranberry sauce	1 8-ounce carton Cool Whip

Combine cream cheese, mayonnaise, and sugar. Add cranberries, pecans, pineapple and vanilla. Fold in Cool Whip. Freeze in muffin tins. Serve with cool whip or mayonnaise.

Fruit Salad

strawberries	2 eggs
cantaloupe	1/2 cup pineapple juice
pineapple	1/2 cup lemon juice
grapes	3/4 cup Splenda

Beat the eggs and cook them with the juices and Splenda until the mixture is thick. Chop the fruit into bite-size pieces. Pour the sauce over the fruit and refrigerate.

Garden Pasta Salad

3	cups uncooked bow-tie pasta	1	cup cherry tomatoes, halved
3	quarts water	4	green onions, sliced
1	cup broccoli flowerets	¼	teaspoon dried oregano
2	small carrots, thinly sliced	¼	teaspoon dried basil
1	14-ounce can artichoke hearts, quartered and drained	½	cup Italian Parmesan dressing

Cook pasta in 3 quarts boiling water for 12 minutes. Add broccoli and carrots to pot, cook for 1 minute, drain. Rinse with cold water to stop cooking process, drain. Put pasta mixture in large bowl. Stir in artichoke hearts and next 4 ingredients. Add dressing, tossing to coat. Cover and chill 2 hours.

4 TO 6 SERVINGS.

Gelatin-Cucumber Salad

1	6-ounce package lime gelatin	3	teaspoons grated onion
1	cup boiling water	2	cucumbers, peeled, seeded, and shredded (about 3 cups)
1	cup plain yogurt	¼	cup lemon juice
2	cups cottage cheese		

Dissolve gelatin in boiling water. Cool to lukewarm. Beat in cottage cheese and yogurt. Fold in remaining ingredients. Pour into a lightly greased mold. Chill until firm.

● ● ● ● ● ● ● ● ● ● ● ●

To unmold, set in warm water for a few minutes.

Salads & Soups

German Cole Slaw

1	head cabbage, slivered	3/4	cup canola oil
1	green pepper, chopped	1	cup sugar
1	large onion, chopped	1	cup apple cider vinegar
3	stalks celery, sliced	1	teaspoon celery seeds
3	carrots, grated	1	teaspoon dry mustard
1	teaspoon salt		

Combine vegetables in large bowl. Set aside. In a small saucepan, bring the remaining ingredients to a boil, and then pour over vegetables, stirring well to coat. Cover and refrigerate several hours or overnight.

Grape Salad

1	8-ounce package cream cheese	2	pounds grapes (red or green)
3/4	cup granulated sugar	1	cup brown sugar
1	8-ounce carton sour cream	1	cup pecans, chopped and
1	teaspoon vanilla		toasted

Mix cream cheese and sugar. In a separate bowl, combine sour cream and 1 teaspoon vanilla. Combine the 2 mixtures and add grapes. Combine brown sugar and nuts and sprinkle over top. Cover and chill overnight.

Layered Taco Salad

1 16-ounce can refried beans
8 green onions, chopped
1 4-ounce can chopped ripe olives, drained
2 medium tomatoes, diced
1 4-ounce can chopped ripe chilies, drained

1 cup shredded Cheddar cheese
1 6-ounce carton avocado dip
1 pound ground beef, sautéed
1 package taco seasoning
  shredded lettuce

Simmer ground beef, drain off fat and mix in taco seasoning. Line bottom of serving dish with shredded lettuce then layer with the above as you like. Serve immediately.

Mom's Famous Frosted Cranberry Salad

1 13½-ounce can crushed pineapple in syrup
2 3-ounce packages lemon gelatin
1 7-ounce bottle ginger ale
1 16-ounce can jellied cranberry sauce

1 2-ounce package Dream Whip
1 8-ounce package cream cheese, softened
½ cup chopped pecans

Drain pineapple and set aside, but reserve the syrup. Add water to the syrup until the mixture equals 1 cup. Heat to boil. Dissolve gelatin in hot liquid and cool in refrigerator or freezer until it is cool to touch. Gently stir in ginger ale and cool until partially set. Whip cranberry sauce with a whisk, blend in pineapple, and fold in gelatin. Put in Pyrex dish and chill until firm.

Topping

Prepare Dream Whip according to package directions. Blend in cream cheese. Spread over mold, and sprinkle with pecans.

Lemon Dressing

1¼ cups olive oil
⅓ cup lemon juice
3 tablespoons Dijon mustard
1½ teaspoons dried basil

1 teaspoon dried oregano
½ teaspoon pepper
¼ teaspoon salt

In a jar with a lid, combine all ingredients, cover tightly and shake vigorously.

Orange Sherbet Gelatin Salad

2 3-ounce packages orange gelatin
1 cup boiling water
1 pint orange sherbet

1 11-ounce can Mandarin oranges, drained
1 cup heavy cream or dessert topping, whipped

Dissolve gelatin in hot water; add sherbet and mix well. When partially set, add orange slices and fold in whipped cream. Pour into 1½-quart mold. Chill until set.

8 SERVINGS.

Pea Salad

3 can peas
½ cup onions
4 boiled eggs, chopped

1 tomato sliced
4 tablespoons mayonnaise
salt and pepper, to taste

Mix all ingredients in a bowl. Chill 1 hour before serving.

Oriental Crunch Salad

2	packages beef flavored ramen noodle soup	1	16-ounce bag coleslaw mix with carrots
1	cup slivered almonds	1	cup olive oil
1	cup sunflower seeds (without shells)	½	cup sugar or sugar substitute
1	bunch green onions, chopped	⅓	cup red wine vinegar

Put small amount of butter or margarine in skillet and toast almonds and sunflower seeds. Put on paper towels and let cool completely. Take noodles from soup mixes and crumble into a large bowl. Add cooled seeds, green onions and coleslaw. Don't mix - noodles should stay on bottom of the bowl. In separate small bowl mix the seasoning packets (from the ramen noodle packages), oil, vinegar and sugar. Pour this mixture over the coleslaw and noodles. Don't mix or stir, cover the bowl and let marinate overnight in refrigerator. Toss well before serving.

Robust Italian Salad

1	16-ounce package salad greens	1	teaspoon Italian seasoning
2½	ounces sliced pastrami, cut into ½-inch pieces	⅓	cup Italian salad dressing
1	cup shredded mozzarella cheese	1	cup seasoned croutons
4	plum tomatoes, chopped		sliced ripe olives, optional

In a large salad bowl, combine first 5 ingredients. Drizzle with dressing; tossing to coat. Top with croutons and olives if desired.

Rice Salad

1	box chicken flavored rice mix	³/₄	teaspoon curry powder
4	chopped green onions	2	6-ounce marinated artichoke
12	stuffed green olives		hearts
¹/₄	cup chopped green peppers	¹/₂	cup mayonnaise

Cook rice as directed omitting the butter. Let cool. In a large bowl, add onions, olives and peppers. Drain artichoke hearts reserving liquid. Combine artichoke hearts with curry powder and mayonnaise. Add rice and toss together with reserved marinade from the artichoke hearts.

Raspberry Salad

2	10-ounce packages frozen raspberries	³/₄	cup boiling water
1	20-ounce can crushed pineapple	1	large package raspberry flavored gelatin
1	6-ounce frozen orange juice thawed		

Drain thawed raspberries and crushed pineapple and save juices. Combine orange juice and 2½ cups liquid. Mix ³/₄ cup boiling water with 1 cup fruit juice and bring to boil. Add gelatin and stir until dissolved. Fold in fruit. Pour in mold and chill.

Salads & Soups

Roasted Vegetable Pasta Salad with Roasted Red Pepper Vinaigrette

1	bunch asparagus	1	clove garlic
1	ear of corn, cut from cob	1-2	tablespoons red wine vinegar
4-5	Roma tomatoes, seeded and roughly chopped	1	tablespoon Dijon mustard
1	small package of fresh white button mushrooms, sliced	1/3-1/2	cup olive oil
			salt and black pepper, to taste
1	small can black olives, sliced	1/4	teaspoon red pepper flakes
1	jar roasted red bell peppers (reserve liquid)	1	pound dry pasta (tri-color Rotini is especially nice for this dish)

Cook pasta in salted boiling water for 7 to 8 minutes, drain and rinse with cold water. Combine the asparagus (cut into bite-sized pieces), tomatoes, corn and mushrooms on a sheet pan. Drizzle vegetables with a small amount of olive oil. Salt and pepper, to taste. Roast vegetables in a 400° oven for 10 to 12 minutes. Take approximately ½ roasted red peppers from jar and slice into thin strips.

Red Pepper Vinaigrette

Put remaining roasted red peppers and clove of garlic in a food processor and purée. Add 1 to 2 teaspoons liquid from jar of peppers, vinegar, and Dijon mustard — pulse in processor to combine. Add red pepper flakes, salt and black pepper, to taste, with processor running, drizzle in ⅓ to ½ cup of olive oil. Combine roasted red peppers, roasted vegetables and pasta in a large bowl and dress with vinaigrette.

Sour Cream and Red Potato Salad

4 hard-boiled eggs	1/3 cup chopped green onions
2/3 cup mayonnaise	3/4 cup chopped celery finely
3/4 cup sour cream	6 cups cooked red potatoes, sliced
1 1/2 teaspoons mustard with horseradish	1/3 cup Italian salad dressing salt, to taste
1/2 pound cooked bacon, crumbled	

Cut eggs in half and remove yolks. In a small bowl, mash yolks and blend with mayonnaise, sour cream, and mustard. In a separate bowl, chop egg whites. Combine with bacon, celery, potatoes, and salad dressing. Fold in mayonnaise mixture and season with salt.

10 SERVINGS.

Spinach Salad

fresh baby spinach	1/4 cup toasted sunflower seeds
1/2 cup blue cheese	Balsamic vinaigrette, to taste
1/2-1 pint strawberries	

Wash completely, spin dry, and then towel dry about 1/2 pound baby spinach. Stem and slice 1/2 to 1 pint strawberries. Add to spinach. Toss with your favorite vinaigrette. Divide among 4 to 6 salad plates. Cut about 1/2 cup blue cheese (Roquefort, Gorgonzola, Amana, Blue d'Auvergne, Stilton. Etc.) in small pieces and add to salads. Top with 1/4 cup toasted sunflower seeds and serve.

Spinach Orange Salad

1 tablespoon olive, vegetable, or hazelnut oil
2 medium radishes, sliced thin
1/2 teaspoon dried marjoram, crumbled
1 green onion, chopped including green tops

pinch of black pepper
1/2 pound fresh spinach, trimmed
pinch of ground nutmeg
1 1/4 tablespoons white wine vinegar
1/2 cup orange slices

In a medium bowl combine the oil, marjoram, pepper and nutmeg. Add orange slices, radishes and green onions. Toss well. Cover and chill in refrigerator for 2 to 3 hours tossing at least twice. Wash spinach, pat it dry and tear into bite-size pieces. Just before serving, add spinach and vinegar to chilled ingredients and toss well.

Strawberry Congealed Salad

2 packages strawberry flavored gelatin
2 cups boiling water
2 bananas, cut up into small bites

1 package frozen strawberries or fresh strawberries if in season
1 8-ounce can crushed pineapple, drained
1 8-ounce carton sour cream

Pour the gelatin packet into the boiling water and dissolve. Add the bananas, strawberries and pineapples into this dissolved gelatin and pour half of this mixture in a 13x9-inch pan. Place this portion into the refrigerator to congeal. Pour the sour cream over this congealed portion and then add the remaining half of the gelatin and fruit mix. Refrigerate one more time to finish congealing the salad.

Strawberry Pretzel Salad

Layer 1

2 cups crushed pretzels	1 stick margarine, melted
½ cup granulated sugar	

Mix together pretzels, sugar and margarine. Press into 9x13-inch baking dish. Bake at 350° for 10 minutes. Let cool in refrigerator.

Layer 2

1 8-ounce package cream cheese, softened	1 cup confectioners' sugar
	1 12-ounce carton whipped topping

Beat cream cheese. Add confectioners' sugar and continue beating. Finally, add whipped topping to cheese and sugar mixture. Spread on top of pretzel layer.

Layer 3

1 6-ounce package strawberry gelatin	2 10-ounce packages frozen strawberries with juice
1⅓ cups boiling water	1 8-ounce tub whipped topping

Dissolve gelatin in boiling water. Partially cool, then add strawberries and let partially set. Spread on top of cheese layer. After gelatin mixture has set top with a layer of whipped topping and serve.

Strawberry Romaine Salad

1 cup vegetable oil
³/₄ cup sugar
¹/₂ cup red wine vinegar
2 cloves garlic, minced
¹/₂ teaspoon salt
¹/₂ teaspoon paprika
¹/₄ teaspoon white pepper

1 bag Romaine lettuce
1 pint strawberries
1 cup shredded Monterey Jack cheese
¹/₂ cup chopped walnuts, toasted at 250° for 20 minutes

Combine first 7 ingredients in large bowl and blend, this is the dressing. Mix the other ingredients and then pour the dressing into the salad mix.

Summer Tabouli

1 cup cracked wheat
4 green onions, chopped
¹/₂ cup chopped parsley
1 cup chopped small mint
¹/₂ cucumber, chopped fine

¹/₂ cup olive oil
1¹/₂ teaspoons salt
¹/₂ teaspoon pepper
1¹/₂ teaspoons ground allspice
juice of 2 lemons

Cover cracked wheat with water and soak at least 1 hour. Wring out by handfuls and put in salad mixing bowl. Add tomatoes, onions, parsley, mint and cucumber. Mix well with olive oil. Add salt, pepper and allspice. Add lemon last, mixing well.

Sweet Chicken Salad

1½ cups coarsely ground cooked
    chicken
¼ cup sweet pickle relish
3 tablespoons mayonnaise

2 tablespoons finely chopped onion
¾ teaspoon salt
¼ teaspoon celery seeds
¼ teaspoon black pepper

Mix all ingredients and refrigerate. Recipe can be doubled.

Veggie Pasta Salad

1 8-ounce package bowtie pasta,
    uncooked
2 cups broccoli flowerets
2 cups sliced fresh carrots

2 cups sliced mushrooms
1 2¼-ounce can sliced black olives
    drained

Cook pasta according to directions, drain and set aside. In a large saucepan, blanch broccoli and carrots in boiling water over high heat for 1 minute. Drain broccoli and carrots and rinse immediately in cold water to stop the cooking process. In a large bowl, combine broccoli, carrots, mushrooms and olives. Add pasta tossing gently to combine. Add Lemon Dressing (page 79); toss well. Cover and chill.

8 SERVINGS.

Watergate Salad

½ cup chopped pecans
1   16-ounce tub whipped topping
1   20-ounce can crushed pineapple,
    drained

½ bag mini marshmallows
1   3.4-ounce box pistachio instant
    pudding

Mix all ingredients together well and refrigerate covered for at least 1 hour prior to serving.

Antipasto Bread

1   16-ounce jar marinated artichoke
    hearts, drained
½ cup sliced deli hard salami,
    chopped
½ cup sliced black olives

2   teaspoons minced garlic
½ cup butter or margarine, melted
1   cup shredded Cheddar cheese
2   11.3-ounce packages refrigerated
    dinner rolls

Preheat oven to 375°. Spray a Bundt pan with non-stick cooking spray.

Chop the artichoke hearts. Mix with the salami, black olives, and garlic. Melt the butter. Separate the dinner rolls and cup them into quarters. Place the cheese into a bowl. Dip 16 dough pieces into the melted butter, then roll in the cheese. Arrange evenly in the pan. Sprinkle with ½ cup of the artichoke mixture. Repeat layers, making the last layer dough pieces. Sprinkle with cheese. Bake 20 to 30 minutes, or until deep golden brown. Cool 5 minutes. Loosen edges of bread from sides of pan with a spatula. Invert bread onto a plate.

Artichoke Bread

2 teaspoons minced garlic	2 cups shredded Cheddar cheese
1 14-ounce can artichoke hearts, drained and chopped	1/2 cup sour cream
	1 loaf unsliced French bread

Preheat the oven to 350°. Mix artichoke hearts, 1½ cups of cheese, sour cream, and garlic. Cut the bread in half lengthwise. Scoop out the center of each half, leaving a ½-inch shell. Crumble the removed pieces of bread and mix them into the artichoke mixture. Spoon this mixture into the shells. Sprinkle the remaining Cheddar cheese on top of each shell. Cover with foil and bake for 25 minutes. Cut into slices.

Artichoke and Oyster Soup

1/2 cup butter	2 16-ounce cans artichoke hearts
1 onion, chopped	1 cup oyster juice
1 bunch green onions, chopped	1 10¾-ounce can cream of mushroom soup
2 garlic cloves, minced	1 bay leaf
2 tablespoons fresh parsley, chopped	salt and pepper, to taste
3 dozen oysters	

Melt butter in pan. Add chopped onions and cook until clear. Add garlic and parsley; cook approximately 2½ minutes. Add oysters, cook another 3 minutes. Add drained, quartered artichoke hearts and cook for a few more minutes. Add oyster liquor, cream of mushroom soup and bay leaf. Cook 20 minutes.

4 SERVINGS.

Baked Potato Soup

4	large baking potatoes	4	green onions, chopped and divided
2/3	cup butter	12	slices bacon, cooked, crumbled, and divided
2/3	cup flour	1 1/4	cups shredded Cheddar cheese, divided
6	cups milk	1	8-ounce carton sour cream
3/4	teaspoon salt		
1/2	teaspoon pepper		

Wash potatoes and prick several times with a fork; bake at 400° for 1 hour or until done. Let cool. Cut potatoes in half lengthwise; scoop out pulp, and set aside. Discard skins. Melt butter in a heavy saucepan over low heat; add flour, stirring until smooth. Cook 1 minute, stirring constantly. Gradually add milk; cook over medium heat, stirring constantly, until mixture is thickened and bubbly. Add potato pulp, salt, pepper, 2 tablespoons green onions, 1/2 cup bacon and 1 cup cheese. Cook until thoroughly heated, and stir in sour cream. Add extra milk, if necessary, for desired consistency. Serve with remaining green onions, bacon, and cheese.

10 CUPS.

Cheesy Vegetable Chowder

10 slices bacon, chopped
1   cup chopped onion
1   cup chopped carrots
2   cans chicken broth
2½ cups diced potatoes
1   package fresh mushrooms, sliced

2   cups milk
1   can whole kernel corn, drained
3   cups shredded Cheddar cheese
3   tablespoons all-purpose flour
    pepper, to taste
    parsley flakes for color

Cook bacon until browned. Add onions and sauté until tender. Add carrots, potatoes, mushrooms, and chicken broth and bring to a boil. Reduce heat; cover and simmer about 25 to 30 minutes or until potatoes are tender. Stir in milk and corn; heat thoroughly. Combine cheese and flour, tossing until cheese is well coated. Add to soup, stir until cheese melts. Season with pepper and parsley flakes, to taste.

Chicken Mexican Soup

1   medium zucchini, chopped
1   can black beans, rinsed and drained
1   can pinto beans, rinsed and drained
1   can whole kernel corn, drained
2   cans chicken broth

1   16-ounce jar thick and chunky mild salsa
3   cups shredded cooked chicken
1   garlic clove, minced
1½ tablespoons chili powder
1   teaspoon cumin

Bring all ingredients to a boil. Reduce heat and simmer for approximately 30 minutes. So easy ... so good!!!

Salads & Soups

Chicken, Oyster and Sausage Gumbo

⅓ cup all-purpose flour
⅓ cup cooking oil
1 large onion, chopped
½ cup green pepper, chopped
4 cloves garlic, minced
½ teaspoon black pepper
2 teaspoons red pepper
4 cups hot water

2 pounds chicken, cut into bite-size pieces
12-ounces Andouille or smoked sausage, cut into bite-size pieces
1 pint oysters
Filé powder

In a heavy 4-quart Dutch oven stir together the flour and oil until smooth. Cook over medium-high heat for 5 minutes, stirring constantly. Reduce heat to medium. Cook and stir the roux constantly about 15 minutes more or until a dark reddish brown roux is formed. Stir in the onion, green pepper, garlic, black pepper, and red pepper. Cook and stir over medium heat for 5 minutes or until vegetables are tender. Gradually stir the hot water into the vegetable mixture. Stir in chicken. Bring mixture to a boil. Reduce heat, cover, and simmer for 40 minutes. Stir in the sausage. Cover and simmer about 20 minutes more or until the chicken is tender. Remove from heat. Skim off fat.

Drain oysters and stir into gumbo. Cover and simmer for 5 minutes more or until oysters are done and mixture is heated through. Serve over hot cooked rice. Serve with ½ teaspoon filé powder to the side of each serving to stir into the gumbo, if desired.

6 SERVINGS.

Chicken Tortilla Soup

1   11-ounce can cream of chicken
    soup
1   can Fiesta Nacho Cheese soup
1   14.5-ounce can diced tomatoes
    and chilies

3   cups milk
1   can green chile enchilada sauce
1   cup cooked chicken, chopped

Mix soups and milk in a pot until hot and well blended. Add enchilada sauce and chicken. Heat to desired temperature and serve.

• • • • • • • • • • • • • • •

Serve with tortilla chips or French bread.

Corn Soup

3   tablespoons butter
1   tablespoon flour
1   medium onion, thinly sliced
    small piece of bay leaf
1/2 cup green peppers, diced
1   teaspoon salt

2   medium potatoes, thinly sliced
1/4 teaspoon pepper
2   cups boiling water
1   19-ounce can cream style corn
2   cups milk, divided

Heat butter in medium saucepan. Add onion and green pepper and cook gently for 3 minutes stirring occasionally. Add potatoes and water to saucepan and bring to a boil. Reduce heat, cover and boil gently for 15 minutes or until potatoes are tender. In a small bowl, mix 1/4 cup of milk with the flour until smooth and stir into boiling mixture. Add remaining milk, bay leaf, salt, pepper and corn. Simmer 15 minutes then discard bay leaf. Mix soup in blender (half at a time) until nearly smooth. Serve hot or chilled.

6 SERVINGS.

Salads & Soups

Dump Soup

1	pound hamburger meat	1	large onion, chopped
3	cans minestrone soup	1	can ranch style beans
2	cans Mexican tomatoes	1	can whole kernel corn
1	can water	2	tablespoons chili powder

Sauté onions. Add beef, then all other ingredients. Cook on low for several hours in a crock pot or on the stove.

Five Can Soup

2	14½-ounce cans black beans	2	pounds ground chuck, cooked and drained
2	16-ounce cans minestrone soup	1	12-ounce can tomato sauce
2	cans Veg-All	½	onion, chopped
1	10¼-ounce can diced tomatoes and green chilies		

Cook ground beef and drain. Add all other ingredients. Stir and simmer for 1 to 2 hours.

8 SERVINGS.

. . . .

Freezes well.

French Onion Soup

4	cups onions, sliced thinly
5	tablespoons butter
1/4	teaspoon pepper
5 1/4	cups water

3	14-ounce cans beef broth
2	14-ounce cans chicken broth
	sliced mozzarella cheese

Sauté the onions in butter until golden brown. Add pepper, water, beef broth and chicken broth. Cook for 1 hour on low heat. Serve soup in bowl, float mozzarella cheese on top.

• • • • • • • • • • • • • • •

Serve croutons or crackers on the side.

Lou's Crab Corn Chowder

1	stick butter
1	bunch chopped green onions
5	10¾-ounce cans cream of mushroom soup
1	quart half-and-half
1	8-ounce package cream cheese

1	16-ounce package frozen white shoe peg corn
1	pound white crabmeat
1	package dry Italian dressing mix
2	caps full Liquid Crab Boil (3 for spicy)

Melt butter, add green onions and sauté until tender. Add soups, stir until creamy. Add half-and-half, stir well. Add seasoning packet and crab boil then cream cheese. Stir to mix again. Add corn and heat thoroughly. Add crabmeat and heat to serving temperature.

• • • • • • • • • • • • • • •

May substitute shrimp for crabmeat if desired.

Salads & Soups

Potato Soup

½	stick unsalted butter	3	10-ounce cans cream of potato soup
4	green onions, chopped	8	ounces processed cheese, cubed
4	celery ribs, chopped	1	12-ounce can kernel corn
1	28-ounce can chicken broth	1	8-ounce container sour cream
1	teaspoon salt		crumbled bacon, optional
½	teaspoon black pepper		shredded cheese, optional

In a saucepan over medium heat, melt the butter. Sauté onions and celery in butter. Add chicken broth, salt, and pepper. Simmer for 30 minutes. Add cream of potato soup, processed cheese, and corn. Stir occasionally until cheese is melted. Do not boil. Fold in sour cream and cook 15 minutes. When serving, top with bacon and shredded cheese.

Seafood Gumbo

½	cup flour	2	pounds shrimp or crawfish, peeled
½	cup oil	1	pound crabmeat
1	large onion, chopped	2	bay leaves
1	clove garlic, minced	2	quarts water
½	bell pepper, chopped		salt and pepper, to taste
¼	cup parsley, chopped		hot cooked rice

Make a roux by mixing the flour in the oil in a large iron skillet over medium heat until brown. Add water very slowly (Caution!), gradually smoothing into a paste. Continue adding all the water. Add vegetables and cook 30 minutes. Add crabmeat. Add bay leaves and all seasonings, but save parsley to end of the cooking time. Cook 15 minutes. Add shrimp. Remove from heat and serve over a large spoonful of rice.

Shrimp and Cheese Soup

1	pound fresh jumbo shrimp	4	tomatoes, peeled and chopped
1	tablespoon butter	1	teaspoon salt
2	tablespoons olive oil	3/4	teaspoon dried oregano
1	medium onion, minced	1/2	teaspoon freshly ground pepper
2	garlic cloves, minced	1	4-ounce package feta cheese, crumbled
1	cup dry white wine		
1	8-ounce bottle clam juice	1/4	cup chopped fresh parsley

Peel shrimp, set aside. Melt butter with olive oil in large saucepan over medium heat. Add onion and garlic; sauté 5 minutes, stirring constantly. Add wine, clam juice, tomatoes, salt, oregano and pepper and bring to a boil. Reduce heat and simmer 10 minutes or until thickened. Stir in cheese and simmer 10 minutes. Add shrimp and cook approximately 5 minutes or until shrimp are cooked. Stir in parsley.

• • • • • • • • • • • • • • • •

1 (3-ounce) log of goat cheese, crumbled, may be substituted for feta cheese.

Strawberry Soup

2/3	cup water	1	pint fresh strawberries
1/3	cup red wine	1/4	cup heavy whipping cream
1/4	cup sugar	1/8	cup sour cream
1	tablespoon fresh lemon juice		

In a medium saucepan, combine water, wine, sugar, and lemon juice. Bring to a boil over medium high heat on and boil uncovered for 15 minutes, stirring occasionally. Wash and dry strawberries. Thinly slice a strawberry lengthwise. Reserve for garnish. Remove tops of remaining strawberries. Purée strawberries. Add purée to boiling mixture, and boil for 10 minutes, stirring frequently. Remove mixture from heat and cool until lukewarm. In a small bowl, combine creams. Fold creams into strawberry mixture. Chill well about 4 hours. Garnish each serving with a slice of Strawberry and serve cold.

2 SERVINGS.

Salads & Soups

Spicy Three Bean Soup

3	boneless chicken breasts	2	teaspoons creole seasoning
3	cups water	1	teaspoon chili powder
1	28-ounce can diced tomatoes, undrained	1	teaspoon paprika
1	10-ounce can frozen cut green beans	¼	teaspoon garlic powder
1	10-ounce can frozen baby lima beans	¼	teaspoon onion powder
1	15-ounce can black beans, drained and rinsed	¼	teaspoon red pepper
			dash hot sauce
			dash soy sauce
			dash Worcestershire sauce

Fill soup pot with 3 cups water. Add chicken breasts, tomatoes, green beans, lima beans and seasonings. Drain and rinse black beans. Cook 30 minutes over medium heat. Remove chicken pieces from soup and cool while soup is still simmering. Shred chicken breasts or cut them into bite-size pieces. Return chicken to soup. Add rinsed and drained black beans to soup. Cook another 10 minutes or until black beans are heated through.

2½ QUARTS.

• • • • • • • • • • • • • •

Freezes well.

Notes

Notes

Main Dishes

Pizza, Casseroles,
Chicken, Beef,
Seafood, Pasta, Pork,
Rice, Quiches, etc.

Artichoke Pizza

2	8-ounce cans crescent rolls	1	4-ounce jar pimento, drained
3/4	cup ranch dressing	3/4	cup shredded mozzarella cheese
1	14-ounce can artichoke hearts, drained and cut	3/4	cup grated Parmesan cheese

Unroll dough and press into a 15x10x1-inch pan. Bake at 375° for 10 minutes.

Combine remaining ingredients, reserving ¼ cup Parmesan cheese. Spread on crust and top with reserved cheese. Bake at 375° for 15 minutes. Let stand for 5 minutes and cut into 2-inch squares.

Rosé Penne

2	tablespoons olive oil	1	teaspoon basil
1	medium onion, thinly sliced	1	cup whipping cream
3	cloves garlic	5	tablespoons chopped Italian parsley
1	pound Italian sausage, casings removed	1	pound penne pasta, boiled in salted water
3/4	cup white wine	1	cup fresh grated Parmesan
1	4½-ounce can Italian style tomatoes		salt and pepper, to taste

Sauté onion in olive oil. Break up sausage and brown with onion. Cook until done; drain grease. Add wine, tomatoes with juice and basil, cook approximately 3 minutes. Add whipping cream and 3 tablespoons parsley; stir until sauce begins to thicken. Add salt and pepper, to taste. Pour sauce over cooked penne and toss with ½ cup of the Parmesan. Sprinkle remaining parsley and Parmesan.

Beef Stroganoff

1	pound sirloin, cut up	1	cup sliced mushrooms
1	cup chopped onion		salt and pepper, to taste
1	clove garlic, chopped	1	8-ounce container sour cream
2	cans beef consommé	1	bag egg noodles
1	tablespoon tomato paste		

Brown steak, sauté onions and garlic; add mushrooms and cook until tender. Add consommé, tomato paste, salt and pepper. Cook egg noodles according to directions on the package. Drain and top noodles with steak mixture and sour cream.

Grandma's Piacante Meatballs

2	pounds ground round beef	2	6-ounce cans tomato sauce
4	eggs	3	cans crushed tomatoes
2	cloves garlic, crushed	3	cans stewed tomatoes
1	cup Italian bread crumbs	1	carrot, whole
3/4	cup Romano cheese		oregano, basil, salt and pepper, to taste
	salt and pepper, to taste		
	pinch of parsley	1	teaspoon sugar
1	onion, chopped		

Using hands mix first 7 ingredients together to make small to medium meatballs. Brown outside of meatball in skillet adding onion to skillet. Add 1 can of tomato sauce and transfer to a large pot with the meatballs. Add remaining can of tomato sauce, crushed tomatoes and stewed tomatoes (about 6 cans). Add carrot (takes away bitter flavor). Add oregano, basil, salt, pepper and sugar. Cover and cook for 3 to 4 hours on low heat. Remove carrot before serving.

Main Dishes

Beef and Pasta

1 pound ground beef
1 medium onion, chopped
1 10³/4-ounce can cream of celery
   soup

¹/4 cup ketchup
1 tablespoon Worcestershire
   sauce
2 cups cooked pasta

Cook beef and onion in medium skillet until beef is done. Drain meat and return to skillet. Add soup, ketchup, Worcestershire sauce and pasta. Heat mixture on low until hot.

4 SERVINGS.

JA Chili

1 tablespoon finely chopped onion
1 tablespoon minced garlic
¹/4 cup vegetable oil
2 pounds ground beef
1 46-ounce can tomato juice

³/4 teaspoon chili powder
¹/2 teaspoon oregano
2 teaspoons salt
¹/4 teaspoon pepper
2 15¹/2-ounce cans kidney beans

Cook onion and garlic in hot oil in a skillet until browned. Add ground beef, and cook until beef is browned, stirring until it crumbles. Add tomato juice and remaining ingredients, and bring to a boil. Reduce heat, and simmer 2 to 3 hours.

The chili actually tastes better after it has chilled overnight and reheated the next day.

Main Dishes

Herbed Rib Roast

¼ cup all-purpose flour	2 teaspoons ground mustard
2 teaspoons garlic pepper or seasoned pepper	1 boneless beef rib roast (4-6 pounds), trimmed and tied
2 tablespoons snipped fresh rosemary	2 teaspoons seasoned salt

In a small bowl, combine the flour and seasonings; rub over roast. Place roast fat side up on a rack in a shallow roasting pan. Bake, uncovered, at 350° for 1¾ to 2¾ hours or until meat reaches the desired doneness. Let stand for 10 to 15 minutes before slicing.

Lasagna

1 pound ground beef	1 24-ounce container cottage cheese
1 clove garlic, minced	1 teaspoon black pepper
3 tablespoons parsley flakes	1 cup Parmesan cheese
4 teaspoons salt	1 pound grated mozzarella cheese
2 cans chopped tomatoes	1 pound grated sharp Cheddar cheese
1½ 8-ounce cans tomato paste	lasagna noodles
1 tablespoon vegetable oil	
2 eggs, beaten	

Cook lasagna noodles in boiling salted water; drain and rinse. Brown meat in oil; add garlic, 1 tablespoon parsley flakes, 2 teaspoons salt, tomatoes, and paste. Simmer 45 minutes. Mix eggs, 2 tablespoons parsley flakes, 2 teaspoons salt, cottage cheese, pepper and Parmesan cheese in a bowl and set aside. Make a layer of noodles in a 13x9x2-inch dish. Cover with half of cottage cheese mixture; add half of the mozzarella cheese and the Cheddar cheese then half of the meat mixture. Repeat for a second layer. Bake at 375° for 30 minutes.

Main Dishes

Parsley Stuffed Flank Steak

1	2-pound flank steak	½	cup minced fresh parsley
4	teaspoons chopped garlic	½	cup grated Romano cheese

Butterfly the flank steak, cutting horizontally from the long side to within ½-inch of opposite side. Open and place on a large piece of heavy-duty aluminum foil (about 18 inches square). Sprinkle parsley, garlic and cheese over meat to within ½-inch of edge. Roll up tightly jelly-roll style, starting with a long side. Wrap tightly in foil. Place in a 13x9x2-inch baking dish. Bake at 325° for 1½ hours or until meat reaches desired doneness (for rare, a meat thermometer should read 140°; medium 160°; well done, 170°). Unwrap and slice steak.

8 SERVINGS.

Chicken Breast Bundles

2	tablespoons butter		garlic and herb cream cheese
4	boneless, skinless chicken breast halves approx. 4-ounces		spread
	salt and pepper	1	8-ounce can crescent rolls

Heat oven to 375°. Lightly spray cookie sheet with non-stick cooking spray. Melt butter in large skillet over medium heat. Sprinkle chicken breast halves with salt and pepper, add to skillet. Cook 8 to 10 minutes or until well browned on both sides. Cool slightly. Separate dough into 4 rectangles. Firmly press perforations to seal. Press each to form 6x4-inch rectangles. Spread cream cheese evenly in center of each rectangle. Place chicken over cheese. Wrap dough around chicken. Press seam to seal. Place on sprayed cookie sheet. Bake at 375° for 18 to 22 minutes or until deep golden brown.

4 SERVINGS.

Main Dishes

Bird's Nest Chicken

6	ounces angel hair pasta	8	ounces Monterey Jack cheese, cubed
4	chicken breasts, skinned and deboned	8	ounces sharp Cheddar cheese, cubed
1	6-ounce can mushrooms	1	teaspoon salt
1	10-ounce package frozen spinach, thawed and drained	½	teaspoon pepper
1	11-ounce can cream of chicken soup	1½	cups croutons

Preheat oven to 375°. Cook angel hair pasta according to box directions. Sprinkle chicken with salt and pepper. Arrange in bottom of square baking dish. Cover chicken with cooked pasta, spinach, and mushroom. Combine the soup with ½ cup of water and bring to a boil. Pour sauce evenly over mushrooms. Bake at 375° for 1 hour. Combine cheeses and croutons and sprinkle over casserole and bake for 5 more minutes.

4 SERVINGS.

Chicken with Cheese Sauce

4-6 chicken breasts		1	8-ounce package cream cheese
1	11-ounce can cream of celery, chicken, or mushroom soup	1	cup shredded Cheddar cheese, optional

Preheat oven to 350°. Cook the chicken breasts (either by boiling or in the microwave). In a saucepan or double boiler, melt the cream cheese and add the soup. Mix well. Add the Cheddar cheese to the soup mixture and stir until the cheese melts.

Place the cooked chicken breasts in an oblong baking dish. Pour the soup mixture over the chicken. If needed, heat for 15 minutes or until all the ingredients are hot. Serve with rice or noodles.

● ● ● ● ● ● ● ● ● ● ● ● ● ● ●

May substitute 1 cup sour cream for cream cheese.

Main Dishes

Chicken and Broccoli Casserole

2	10-ounce packages frozen broccoli
3-4	chicken breasts, cooked and cut into bite-sized pieces
2	10³/₄-ounce cans cream of chicken soup
³/₄	cup mayonnaise
³/₄	teaspoon lemon juice
³/₄	teaspoon curry powder
¹/₂	cup shredded sharp Cheddar cheese
	bread crumbs

Cook the broccoli and drain; arrange in a greased 9x13-inch baking dish. Place the chicken on top of broccoli. Mix the soup, mayonnaise, lemon juice and curry powder together. Pour over chicken; sprinkle with cheese and top with bread crumbs. Bake at 350° for 30 minutes or until thoroughly heated. This dish can be made ahead of time and kept in refrigerator. Allow extra heating time if made ahead.

Chicken Spaghetti

1	fryer, boiled and deboned
1	cup chopped onion
¹/₂	cup chopped bell pepper
¹/₂	cup chopped celery
¹/₂	cup margarine
1	small jar pimento, diced
1	11-ounce can cream of chicken soup
1	10³/₄-ounce can cream of mushroom soup
1	8-ounce package spaghetti cooked in the chicken broth
1	pound processed cheese cut into cubes

Sauté onion, bell pepper, and celery in margarine until tender. In a large bowl, mix all ingredients and toss well. Pour into a greased baking dish. Bake at 350° for 45 minutes or until hot through center.

6 TO 8 SERVINGS.

Main Dishes

Chicken Enchiladas

1	tablespoon butter	1	cup Cheddar cheese
½	cup sour cream	1	10¾-ounce can cream of mushroom soup
½	cup chopped green onions		
1½	cups cooked diced breast meat	6	12-inch flour tortillas
½	teaspoon garlic powder	¼	cup milk
1	4-ounce can diced green chilies		

Preheat oven to 350°. Lightly grease large casserole dish.

In a medium saucepan over medium heat, melt the butter and sauté the green onion until tender (about 4 minutes). Add the garlic powder, stir in the green chilies, cream of mushroom soup and sour cream. Mix well. Set aside ¾ of this sauce in a bowl. To the remaining ¼ of the sauce still in the pan add the cooked chicken and ½ of the Cheddar cheese. Stir together. Fill each tortilla with the chicken mixture and roll up. Place seam side down in the prepared casserole dish. Combine the milk with the ¾ of the sauce that was reserved. Spoon this over the rolled tortillas and top with the remaining cheese. Bake in preheated oven at for 30 to 35 minutes.

Chicken Spectacular

3	cups diced cooked chicken	1	14.5-ounce can French style green beans, drained
1	package cooked wild and white rice		
		1	cup mayonnaise
1	can cream of celery soup	1	package almonds, optional
1	chopped medium onion		salt and pepper, to taste
			grated Cheddar cheese

Heat oven to 350°. Mix all ingredients together then pour into buttered 3-quart casserole. Spread grated cheese over top. Bake about 25 to 30 minutes.

8 SERVINGS.

Main Dishes

Chicken Paprikash

4	large boneless chicken breasts, halved	1/2	teaspoon pepper
1	stick butter		Paprika
1	medium onion	1	18-ounce container sour cream
1/2	teaspoon crushed garlic		cornstarch

In a large saucepan, melt butter and sauté onions with garlic until they begin to soften, set aside. Cook chicken until white on both sides, stir together with the onions and garlic. Add pepper. Add in paprika, lightly covering one side of the chicken. Stir all together until paprika is dissolved into butter and forms a reddish sauce. Reduce heat, cover and simmer for 45 minutes to 1 hour, stirring every 15 minutes. Remove chicken when tender, leaving sauce and onions in pan. Slowly add sour cream to sauce, constantly stirring to dissolve thoroughly. Add 1/2 to 1 teaspoon cornstarch dissolved in water to keep sauce from separating. Serve chicken over rice or egg noodles with sauce served on the side to pour over.

Chicken Picatta and Fresh Steamed Spinach

2 boneless chicken breasts (flattened with rolling pin between layers of plastic wrap)
  salt and pepper, to taste
2 tablespoons olive oil
¼ cup white wine

2 tablespoons capers
  juice of 1 lemon
2 tablespoons butter
2 packages fresh spinach, steamed

Add olive oil to hot skillet. Season chicken breasts with salt and pepper and sauté until brown and cooked through. Remove from pan and set aside. Add white wine to pan to deglaze. Stir and cook for a couple of minutes. Add lemon juice and stir until thickened. Add capers. Then add butter. Stir together and pour over chicken. Serve over a bed of steamed fresh spinach.

Chicken Tetrazzini

1 16-ounce package spaghetti noodles
1 large can chicken chunks
1 10¾-ounce can chicken broth
1 teaspoon celery salt
1½ cups mozzarella cheese
½ cup Cheddar cheese

1 10¾-ounce can cream of mushroom soup
1 10¾-ounce can roasted garlic soup
1 large onion
1 6-ounce jar sliced mushrooms, drained

Cook spaghetti noodles according to the package directions; drain. Return noodles to pot, and toss with chicken broth. Stir together chicken and next 8 ingredients. Spoon mixture into a lightly greased 13x9-inch baking pan. Bake, covered, at 350° for 30 minutes; uncover and bake 5 more minutes or until cheese is melted and bubbly.

Main Dishes

Chicken Wellington

4	6-ounce boneless skinless chicken breast halves	2	15-ounce packages refrigerated pie pastry
1/4	teaspoon salt	1	teaspoon dried rosemary, crushed
1	tablespoon olive oil		
1/4	teaspoon pepper	1	egg, lightly beaten
2	tablespoons butter, softened, divided	1/2	teaspoon rubbed sage

Sauce

1 1/4	teaspoons chicken bouillon granules	2	tablespoons white wine or chicken broth
3	tablespoons all-purpose flour	2	tablespoons butter
1 1/4	cups hot water		

Flatten chicken to 1/4-inch thickness. In a large skillet, cook chicken in oil and 1 tablespoon butter for 4 to 5 minutes on each side until juices run clear. Meanwhile, in a small bowl, combine the rosemary, sage, salt, pepper and remaining butter. Unroll pastry sheets; cut each into a 9-inch square. Discard scraps. Place chicken breast half on each square; spread chicken with butter mixture. Fold pastry over chicken. Trim off excess pastry; pinch seams to seal. Place on greased baking sheet; brush with egg. Bake at 450° for 18 to 20 minutes or until golden brown. Let stand 10 minutes before serving. Meanwhile, dissolve bouillon in hot water. In a small saucepan, melt butter; stir in flour until smooth. Gradually stir in bouillon broth and wine or chicken broth. Bring to a boil; cook and stir for 2 minutes or until thickened. Serve with the chicken.

Main Dishes

Chicken with Artichoke Hearts

4	boneless, skinless chicken breasts	½	pound mushrooms, sliced
1	teaspoon salt	¼	cup flour
½	teaspoon pepper	1½	cups chicken broth
1	teaspoon paprika	½	cup white wine
¾	cup butter or margarine, divided	1	15-ounce can artichoke hearts, quartered

Sprinkle chicken with salt, pepper, and paprika. Melt 4 tablespoons butter in skillet over medium heat, brown chicken on all sides and place in a shallow casserole. Place remaining butter in skillet and cook mushrooms gently for a few minutes; add flour and stir until will blended. Stir in chicken broth and wine; cook over medium heat, stirring constantly, until mixture is smooth and slightly thickened. Drain artichoke hearts and arrange among chicken pieces. Pour sauce over chicken and artichokes. Bake at 350° for 45 minutes to 1 hour.

Chicken with Lime Sauce

1	teaspoon salt	½	teaspoon thyme
1	teaspoon pepper	1	pound boneless skinless chicken tenders
¼	teaspoon red pepper		
¼	teaspoon paprika	2	tablespoons butter
1	teaspoon garlic powder	2	tablespoons olive oil
½	teaspoon onion powder	4	tablespoons lime juice

In a bowl, mix together the dry spices. Sprinkle mixture on both sides of chicken breasts with a spoon. In a skillet heat butter and olive oil together over medium high heat. Sauté chicken until golden brown on each side, about 5 minutes. Add lime juice to chicken and stir until chicken is coated.

2 TO 4 SERVINGS.

Main Dishes

Crock Pot
Cheesy Chicken Casserole

2	10-ounce package frozen broccoli spears, thawed	1½	cups grated Parmesan cheese
1	teaspoon salt	10-12	slices cooked chicken or turkey
2	cups milk	2	8-ounce packages cream cheese
1	teaspoon garlic salt		

Cut broccoli spears into bite-size pieces and place in bottom of greased crock pot. In a saucepan, blend milk, cream cheese, Parmesan cheese, salt and garlic salt over low heat until melted and smooth. Pour 1 cup over broccoli, top with sliced chicken. Pour remaining sauce over chicken. Cover and cook on LOW 4 to 6 hours.

4 TO 6 SERVINGS.

Ellie's *Easy But Good* Chicken

2	chickens cut up and boned (leave bone in thighs and legs)	1	cup white wine
2	10¾-ounce cans condensed cream of mushroom soup	1	pint sour cream
			paprika

Mix soup, sour cream and wine together. Pour over chicken placed in 9x13-inch flat baking dish. Sprinkle generously with paprika. Bake at 350° for approximately 1 to 1½ hours or until tender. Best if cooked a little ahead of serving time. Allow to cool, then reheat for serving.

Main Dishes

Garlic Chicken

1	3- to 3½-pound chicken, cut into 8 pieces, rinsed and patted dry	1	teaspoon dried rosemary, crumbled
	salt and pepper, to taste	1	teaspoon dried oregano
3	tablespoons olive oil	½	cup dry white wine
5	garlic cloves, minced	1	teaspoon hot pepper sauce
		½	teaspoon Worcestershire sauce

Sprinkle chicken with salt and pepper, to taste. In a large skillet, heat the oil over medium heat. Add the chicken and cook over medium-high heat, turning once or twice, for about 6 minutes, until browned on both sides. Reduce the heat to low, cover, and cook for about 25 minutes, until the chicken juices run clear when a thigh is pierced. Remove with a slotted spoon to a plate. Add the garlic, rosemary, and oregano to the skillet and cook over medium-low heat, stirring frequently, for about 2 minutes. Add the wine and bring to a boil over high heat, stirring to scrape up any bits from the bottom of the pan. Gently boil the sauce for 2 to 3 minutes, until it has thickened slightly. Stir in the hot-pepper sauce and add Worcestershire sauce. Return the chicken to the skillet and cook over low heat to warm through. Serve the chicken with the sauce spooned over it.

Imperial Chicken

4	boneless, skinless chicken breasts	³/₄	cup Parmesan cheese
2	sticks margarine	¹/₄	cup parsley flakes
2	cups bread crumbs (make your own from white bread)	2	teaspoons garlic salt
		¹/₈	teaspoon pepper

Preheat oven to 350°. Mix bread crumbs, Parmesan cheese, parsley flakes, garlic salt and pepper. Melt margarine and dip chicken in it. Roll dipped chicken in crumb mixture.

Place on Pyrex dish and bake 1 hour at 350°.

Italian Chicken

6	chicken breasts skinned and boned	¹/₂	teaspoon dried crushed tarragon
¹/₂	cup Italian salad dressing	¹/₃	cup grated Parmesan cheese
¹/₄	teaspoon black pepper		fresh tarragon

Preheat oven to 350°. Place chicken in a 12x7½x2-inch baking dish. Fill dish with ¼-inch of water. Pour dressing over chicken and sprinkle with black pepper, tarragon and Parmesan cheese. Bake 20 to 30 minutes. Garnish with fresh tarragon.

6 SERVINGS.

Main Dishes

One Pan Sage, Onion, Chicken and Sausage

1	large onion or 2 small	1	4-pound chicken, cut into 10 pieces
½	cup olive oil, not extra virgin		
2	teaspoons English mustard	12	sausage, Italian, sweet
1	tablespoons dried sage	2	tablespoons sage leaves, chopped
	pepper, ground		
1	lemon	¼	cup red wine vinegar
1	tablespoons Worcestershire sauce	¼	cup sweet cherry peppers

Peel and cut the onion into eighths, and put into a freezer bag with the oil, mustard, dried sage, a good grinding of pepper, the lemon juice, the squeezed out rinds cut into eighths and the Worcestershire sauce. Squish everything around to mix (the mustard needs help to combine) and then add the chicken pieces. Leave to marinate in the refrigerator overnight, or for up to 2 days. Preheat the oven to 425°. Allow the chicken to come to room temperature in its marinade. Arrange the chicken pieces in a roasting pan, skin side up, with the marinade, including all the bits and pieces, and tuck the sausages around them. Sprinkle the fresh sage leaves over the chicken and sausages and then put the pan into the oven to cook for 1 hour and 15 minutes. Turn the sausages over halfway through to color them evenly. Twenty minutes before it is done, add the red wine vinegar and the sweet cherry peppers. Arrange the chicken and sausages on a large platter.

6 SERVINGS.

Main Dishes

Oriental Chicken

4   chicken breasts, cooked and cut into bite-size pieces
1   package wild rice, cooked as directed
1   11-ounce can cream of celery soup, undiluted
1   onion, chopped
1   cup mayonnaise
1   4-ounce can mixed Chinese vegetables
1   2-ounce jar pimentos
1   16-ounce can French styles beans drained
    salt and pepper, to taste

Mix above ingredients. Salt and pepper, to taste. Bake at 350° until bubbly.

8 SERVINGS.

Pecan Chicken Fingers

6   skinned and boned chicken breasts
1   cup all-purpose flour
1½ cups pecans, toasted and ground
¼   cup sesame seeds
¾   teaspoon salt
⅛   teaspoon pepper
1   egg, lightly beaten
1   cup buttermilk
½   cup melted butter

Cut chicken into 4 to 6 strips each. Combine flour and next 4 ingredients, set aside. Combine egg and buttermilk. Dip chicken strips into buttermilk mixture; dredge in flour mixture. Pour butter into 15x10-inch pan, add chicken, turn to coat both sides. Bake at 375° for 30 minutes.

Main Dishes

Parmesan Chicken

1½ cups Italian bread crumbs	6 chicken breast, boneless and skinless
½-¾ cup grated Parmesan cheese	
1 teaspoon pepper	1-2 sticks butter, melted
½-1 tablespoon salt	

Preheat oven to 350°. Mix bread crumbs, cheese, salt and pepper in a bowl. Pound chicken slightly if needed, and dip in melted butter and then crumb and cheese mixture. Place on baking dish or on cookie sheet. Cook until juices run clear.

Poppy Seed Chicken

6 chicken breast boiled and chopped into chunks (or 2-3 cans of chunk chicken)	2 11-ounce cans cream of chicken soup
	poppy seeds
1 8-ounce container sour cream	1 roll of buttery crackers, crushed

Mix chicken, sour cream and soups in a large bowl. Butter 9x13-inch dish and pour mixture into pan. Sprinkle poppy seeds evenly on top of mixture. Top with crushed crackers. Melt 1½ sticks butter and sprinkle on top of casserole. Bake at 350° for 35 to 40 minutes or until bubbly.

• • • • • • • • • • • • • • • •

Great to eat alone or as a topping for pasta or rice.

Main Dishes

Portuguese Roasted Chicken and Potatoes

3 cups water
1 tablespoon good red wine vinegar
1 tablespoon paprika
1 teaspoon salt
1 tablespoon fresh ground pepper
1 medium onion, chopped

1 tomato, chopped
3 tablespoons fresh chopped parsley
4 Idaho potatoes
1 Chorizo (Portuguese sausage) may substitute Kielbasa if you don't have Chorizo

Preheat oven to 375°. Pour water into a roasting pan. Add vinegar, to taste. The water should have just a hint of vinegary taste. Sprinkle paprika over the water and mix, removing the lumps. Add salt, pepper, onion, tomato, parsley and potatoes. Before cooking add Chorizo or Kielbasa. Bake for 2 hours. Do not cover potatoes or let them touch because they will steam and not roast. The potatoes will have a nice red color when they are done.

Roasted Chicken

1 package dry Italian salad dressing mix (unprepared)
¼ cup oil
⅓ cup vinegar
2 tablespoons water

¼ teaspoon Italian seasoning blend
1 whole roasting chicken (approximately 5 pounds)
1 pinch paprika
1 pinch Italian seasoning blend

Preheat oven to 375°. This recipe is made in a clay cooker. To prepare the cooker, soak the cover for 15 minutes, and spray the bottom with any non-stick coating. Mix first 5 ingredients, set aside. Wash the chicken and pat it dry. Put chicken in cooker and pour salad dressing mixture on top, then use hands to rub it all over the chicken skin. Lightly sprinkle entire chicken with paprika (a pinch or so), then sprinkle a pinch or so of the dry Italian seasoning on top as well. Cover and cook at 375° for 2 hours. About 1 to 1½ hours into the cooking time, check the chicken. If there is liquid half-way up the chicken

Main Dishes

Portuguese Roasted Chicken and Potatoes – continued

or more, drain all of the liquid so that the chicken is dry enough to roast, then continue cooking. If it's not halfway up the chicken, just leave whatever juices are in there and continue cooking.

4 SERVINGS.

Swiss Chicken Quiche

1	cup shredded Swiss cheese	2	eggs, beaten
2	tablespoons all-purpose flour	¼	cup chopped onion
1	tablespoon instant chicken bouillon	2	tablespoons pimento
2	cups cooked chicken, shredded	2	tablespoons chopped bell pepper
1	cup milk	1	9-inch unbaked pie shell

Preheat oven to 425°. Prick bottom and sides of pie shell. Bake about 8 minutes. Remove pie shell from oven and reduce oven to 350°. Toss cheese with flour and bouillon in medium bowl. Add chicken, milk, eggs, onion, pimento and bell pepper. Pour into baked pie shell. Bake approximately 45 minutes or until set. Cool about 10 minutes before slicing.

Main Dishes

Rotel Chicken Casserole

4	chicken breasts	½	bell pepper, optional
6	ounces vermicelli pasta		mushrooms, optional
4	cups water	1	can Rotel tomatoes, diced
1	onion	1	pound processed cheese, cut up

Preheat oven to 350°. Cook the chicken. Remove chicken from the water and add the vermicelli to the water. Cook until the vermicelli is done, do not drain. Chop the chicken breasts. Add the Rotel and the processed cheese to the vermicelli. Stir until the cheese is melted. Add the chicken and onions to the mixture. Pour into a 9x13-inch baking dish.

Bake for 20 to 30 minutes.

Tricia's Quick and Easy Bar-B-Que Chicken

6-8	chicken parts, skin on (dark meat is better)	1	onion, quartered
1	18-ounce bottle of barbecue sauce	1	orange cut into slices
		1	12-ounce can Coke
			salt and pepper

Place chicken pieces in bottom of Dutch oven. Sprinkle with salt and pepper. Pour Coke over chicken pieces. Add onion and orange slices. Pour barbecue sauce over all ingredients making sure all pieces of chicken are covered. More Coke or barbecue sauce may be added if necessary. Bring to boil. Cover, reduce heat. Simmer for 30 to 35 minutes or until tender and cooked through.

Main Dishes

Baked Jambalaya

1	stick butter, melted	1	pound uncooked chicken breast
1	pound smoked sausage, sliced	1	bunch green onions, chopped
1	can tomatoes and green chilies	2	cups raw converted rice
1	can French onion soup	2	bay leaves
1	can beef consommé		

Mix all ingredients and pour into a buttered 9x13-inch casserole dish. Cover and bake 1 hour at 350° then stir and bake an additional 30 minutes or until all liquid is absorbed.

Barbecue Shrimp

2	pounds unpeeled shrimp	3	teaspoons red pepper
1	cup salted butter	1	teaspoon dried basil
1	cup vegetable oil	1	teaspoon oregano
4	teaspoons minced garlic	1½	teaspoons paprika
2	teaspoons dried crushed rosemary	1	teaspoon salt
5	whole bay leaves	1	teaspoon black pepper
		2	teaspoons lemon juice

Melt butter; add oil and all other ingredients, except shrimp. Stir over medium heat until bubbly. Reduce heat, simmer for 8 minutes. Add shrimp simmer for 8 minutes. Shrimp is done when pink through.

Main Dishes

Baked Company Shrimp

4	pounds headless shrimp, peeled and deveined	5	cloves garlic
1	10-ounce bottle Italian dressing	1	bunch green onions
1	tablespoon parsley	2	tablespoons Worcestershire sauce

Marinate cleaned shrimp in Italian dressing for at least 3 hours. Preheat oven to 350°. Place all ingredients in a 9x13-inch glass dish. Stir well and bake for 20 to 30 minutes. Test after 20 minutes.

8 SERVINGS.

Bar-B-Q Shrimp

4	pounds large unpeeled shrimp		Creole seasoning, to taste
2	sticks melted butter	4	lemons
1/4	cup olive oil	1/2	cup barbecue sauce
	garlic salt, to taste	1/2	cup rum
	celery salt, to taste		Black pepper

Place unpeeled shrimp in heavy pan. Mix together remaining ingredients to make sauce and pour on shrimp. Sprinkle heavily with black pepper. Place shrimp under broiler on lower rack for about 6 minutes. Stir and place back under broiler for about 5 more minutes.

6 SERVINGS

Broiled Spicy Creole Shrimp

1½ tablespoons spicy Creole
    seasoning
1½ tablespoons paprika

½ cup unsalted butter, melted
1 pound large peeled shrimp

Spicy Creole Seafood Seasoning

1 tablespoon paprika
1 tablespoon salt
2 teaspoons onion powder
2 teaspoons garlic powder
1 teaspoon red pepper

1 teaspoon white pepper
1 teaspoon black pepper
2 teaspoons dried thyme
2 teaspoons dried oregano
2 teaspoons dried basil

Combine seasoning with paprika. Add half of spice mixture to butter and stir. Coat shrimp in butter mixture and place in a single layer large foil lined pan. Pour any remaining butter mixture over shrimp. Broil close to high heat until pink, 3 to 5 minutes.

½ CUP SPICY CREOLE SEAFOOD SEASONING
2 SERVINGS BROILED SPICY CREOLE SHRIMP.

Easy Étouffée

4 tablespoons butter
1 cup chopped onion
½ cup chopped celery
½ cup green onion
3 cloves garlic, minced
2 tablespoons all-purpose flour

¾ cup chicken broth
1 pound shrimp, peeled or 1 pound
    crawfish tails, cleaned
    salt and pepper, to taste
    hot pepper sauce, to taste
    Cajun seasoning, to taste
    hot cooked rice

Melt butter in a 2-quart baking dish. Add onion and next 3 ingredients. Cover and microwave on high 3 to 5 minutes, stirring occasionally. Cook just until vegetables are translucent. Stir in flour and chicken broth and microwave on high for 4 minutes. Add shrimp/crawfish and remaining ingredients. Cover and microwave on high for 4 additional minutes. Serve over rice.

Main Dishes

Herbed Shrimp and Feta Casserole

2	large eggs	1	teaspoon dried oregano
1	cup evaporated milk	4	cloves garlic, minced
1	cup plain yogurt	½	pound angel hair pasta, cooked
1	18-ounce package crumbled feta cheese	1	16-ounce jar mild chunky salsa
⅓	pound shredded Swiss cheese	1½	pounds medium shrimp, cooked and peeled
⅓	cup chopped fresh parsley	¼	pound shredded mozzarella cheese
1	teaspoon dried basil		

Preheat oven to 350°. Coat bottom and sides of 8x12-inch baking dish with cooking spray. In separate bowl, blend first 9 ingredients together. Spread half of pasta over bottom of baking dish, cover with salsa and add half of the shrimp. Spread remaining pasta over shrimp, pour and spread egg mixture over pasta. Add remaining shrimp and top with mozzarella cheese. Bake 30 minutes. Remove from oven and let stand 10 minutes before serving.

Key Lime Shrimp Over Rice

1	cup jasmine rice	4	green onions
1	pound raw, medium, peeled shrimp or 1 pound raw scallops		juice of 2 limes
4	tablespoons olive oil, divided	3	tablespoons chopped fresh cilantro
3	cloves garlic, chopped		

Prepare rice according to package directions. Sauté shrimp in 2 tablespoons olive oil; drain. In another skillet, sauté garlic and green onions in remaining olive oil. Add shrimp, lime juice, and cilantro. Serve over steamed jasmine rice.

4 SERVINGS.

• • • • • • • • • • • • • • •

For an oriental flare, add chopped fresh ginger. May substitute scallops for shrimp.

Main Dishes

Grilled Salmon
with Tomato Herb Relish

4	10-ounce salmon fillets, skin removed

salt and pepper, to taste
3 tablespoons olive oil

Tomato Herb Relish

3 Roma tomatoes, finely diced
2 tablespoons chopped fresh dill
2 tablespoons chopped fresh parsley

2 tablespoons finely chopped red onion
3 tablespoons white wine
1 tablespoon lemon juice
½ teaspoon Worcestershire sauce
½ teaspoon minced garlic

Preheat grill to high. Combine 1 tablespoon of the olive oil with all the relish ingredients in a bowl and set aside. Rub the salmon fillets with the remaining 2 tablespoons olive oil and season both sides generously with salt and pepper. Place the salmon on the hot grill and cook each side for about 4 minutes, until the fish is still a bit undercooked in the center (overcooking will dry it out). Remove the fish from the grill, spoon the tomato herb relish over each piece.

Pesto Crusted Salmon

salmon	pesto
thinly sliced tomatoes, optional	bread crumbs, dry

Use as large a filet as you want, salt and pepper, cover with the sliced tomatoes (if using), ¼-inch pesto, then bread crumbs. Cover with plastic wrap and refrigerate overnight. Bake at 425° for 15 to 18 minutes, depending on thickness of the fish, if allowed to come to room temperature before going in the oven.

• • • • • • • • • • • • • • •

This was served at room temperature at a cocktail party and was a major hit.

• • • • • • • • • • • • • • •

Use some sun-dried tomato Bruschetta in place of bread crumbs.

Shrimp Creole

½	cup canola oil	1	tablespoon paprika
1	cup chopped green pepper	1	teaspoon salt
2	cups chopped onion	3	cups water
1	cup sliced celery	1	bay leaf
2	teaspoons minced fresh garlic	3	pounds shrimp, peeled and
2	cups canned whole tomatoes		deveined

Heat oil and sauté the vegetables until tender. Add tomatoes and simmer 5 minutes. Stir in paprika, red pepper, salt, water, and bay leaf; simmer 15 minutes. Add shrimp and simmer 10 to 12 more minutes or until shrimp are done. Serve over hot white rice.

Main Dishes

Shrimp and Andouille Spaghetti

3	stalks celery	2	pounds peeled shrimp
2	sticks butter	1½	pounds andouille sausage cubed, cooked and drained
3	onions, chopped		
1	bell pepper, chopped	1	pound processed cheese
1	teaspoon chopped garlic	1	pint half-and-half
⅓	cup flour		Creole seasoning, to taste
1	bunch green onions, chopped		angel hair pasta
½	cup chopped parsley	8	ounces grated Cheddar cheese

Sauté onions, bell pepper, garlic and celery in butter. Cook until soft. Slowly stir in flour. Add green onions. Add cheese, half-and-half, andouille which has been cooked and drained, and shrimp and seasoning to taste. Cook 15 to 20 minutes. Add cooked pasta. Spread in baking dish and top with grated Cheddar cheese. Bake at 350° until cheese is melted.

12 SERVINGS.

Shrimp Spaghetti

1	pound jumbo shrimp	2	tablespoons flour
	seasoning packet from Kraft spaghetti mix (green box)	2	cups milk
		¼	cup butter
1	cup chopped celery		

Boil shrimp in crab boil seasoning. Sauté celery in butter until soft. Add flour and seasoning. Slowly add milk (will be soupy). Cook over medium heat stirring frequently. Add shrimp when sauce is thickened. Salt and pepper, to taste. Serve with pasta.

Main Dishes

Shrimp Enchiladas

2   pounds fresh shrimp, boiled,
      peeled and coarsely chopped
1   10-ounce can cream of shrimp
      soup, undiluted
1   10-ounce can cream of onion
      soup, undiluted
1   cup picante sauce
1   8-ounce package cream cheese,
      softened

½   cup sour cream
2   cups shredded Monterey Jack
      cheese
9   green onions, chopped
1   4½-ounce can chopped green
      chilies
10 6-inch flour tortillas
      fresh cilantro for garnish

Boil, peel and coarsely chop fresh shrimp. Set aside. Combine soups and picante sauce in saucepan over medium heat, stirring often until thoroughly heated. Spoon 1 cup of mixture into bottom of a lightly greased 13x9-inch dish; reserve remaining mixture and keep warm. Beat cream cheese and sour cream with electric mixer until smooth; stir in shrimp, 1 cup Monterey Jack cheese, green onions and chilies. Heat the tortillas according to package directions. Spoon 3 to 4 tablespoons of shrimp mixture down center of each tortilla and place seam side down in baking dish. Pour remaining soup mixture over enchiladas; top with remaining 1 cup Monterey Jack cheese. Bake at 350° for approximately 45 minutes. Garnish.

• • • • • • • • • • • • • • •

You may use 2 cups of cooked, chopped chicken for shrimp.

Main Dishes

Shrimp Florentine

1 32-ounce package frozen chopped spinach, thawed and drained
2 pounds medium shrimp, cooked and peeled
½ cup all-purpose flour
1 cup dry wine

1 18-ounce package shredded Cheddar cheese
   lemon pepper, to taste
½ cup unsalted butter
1 medium onion, chopped
1½ cups half-and-half
2 teaspoons paprika vegetable cooking spray

Preheat oven to 325°. Coat 9x13-inch dish with vegetable spray. Drain spinach well and blot moisture out of shrimp. Add lemon pepper to spinach. Spread spinach over bottom of dish and layer shrimp over spinach. In a saucepan, sauté onions in butter until soft. Add flour, and then gradually blend in half-and-half, stirring until thickened. Slowly stir in wine and then add salt, pepper and paprika. Pour over shrimp and sprinkle with cheese. Bake uncovered for 30 minutes. Allow to rest several minutes before serving.

10 SERVINGS.

Shrimp and Sausage Jambalaya

1 cup long-grain rice	2 cloves garlic, minced
4 cups water	2 tablespoons butter
½ cup crab boil seasoning	1 16-ounce can tomatoes, chopped
1 pound large shrimp, peeled and deveined	1½ 8-ounce cans tomato paste
	⅓ cup water
1 cup chopped celery	1 teaspoon Worcestershire sauce
½ cup chopped onion	2 cups chopped smoked sausage

Cook rice according to package, set aside. In a large saucepan, combine water and crab boil seasoning. Bring to a boil. Reduce heat, cover and simmer mixture for 15 minutes. Add shrimp, return to boiling, reduce heat and simmer about 3 minutes or until shrimp turn pink. In a 3-quart saucepan cook celery, onion, and garlic in butter until vegetables are tender. Stir in the **undrained** tomatoes, tomato paste, water and Worcestershire sauce. Bring to a boil. Reduce heat, cover, and simmer for about 15 minutes. Stir in cooked rice, shrimp, and sausage to tomato mixture. Cook, uncovered until mixture is heated through, stirring occasionally.

6 SERVINGS.

Crab Imperial

6 ounces fresh lump crabmeat	3 tablespoons grated Parmesan cheese
1 teaspoon lemon juice	butter and paprika
½ cup mayonnaise	
2 teaspoons fresh grated parsley	

Toss crabmeat, lemon juice mayonnaise, and parsley. Place in crab shells or baking dish. Brush with butter and sprinkle with paprika and grated cheese. Bake 10 minutes in a 350° oven, then place under broiler for 2 to 3 minutes.

6 SERVINGS.

Main Dishes

Speedy Scampi

⅓	cup butter	1¾	pounds large fresh shrimp, peeled and deveined
2	green onions, sliced	½	cup chopped fresh parsley
4	large garlic cloves, minced	½	teaspoon hot sauce
½	cup fresh lemon juice	12	ounces angel hair pasta, cooked
½	teaspoon salt		

Melt butter in a large skillet over medium-high heat; add green onions, minced garlic, lemon juice, and salt; cook garlic mixture 2 to 3 minutes or until bubbly. Reduce heat to medium; add shrimp, and cook, stirring constantly, 5 minutes or just until shrimp turn pink. Stir in parsley and hot sauce. Toss with hot pasta.

JA Crabcakes

2	tablespoons butter	1	tablespoon freshly minced parsley
1	pound fresh crabmeat	1½	teaspoons Old Bay seasoning
6-8	saltine crackers, finely crushed	½	teaspoon dry mustard
½	cup mayonnaise	½	teaspoon pepper
1	egg, slightly beaten	½	teaspoon salt

Drain crabmeat. Combine crackers and next 7 ingredients, gently fold in crabmeat. Make 8 thin round patties. Melt butter in skillet over medium heat. Cook patties 4 to 5 minutes on each side or until golden brown.

Main Dishes

Shrimp Rotini Casserole

1	10-ounce can diced chilies and tomatoes	1	egg, slightly beaten	
2	cups shredded sharp Cheddar cheese	1/2	teaspoon pepper paprika	
2	cups cooked shrimp	1	cup ricotta cheese	
1	18-ounce container sour cream	3/4	teaspoon salt	
		1	18-ounce package rotini, cooked	

Stir together first 8 ingredients in a large bowl; stir in cooked rotini pasta. Spoon mixture into a lightly greased 2-quart dish and sprinkle with paprika. Bake at 350° for 45 minutes. Let stand 10 to 15 minutes before serving.

4 TO 6 SERVINGS.

Snapper Cat Island

8	grilled, blackened or fried snapper filets (any fish will do)	1/2	pound small peeled shrimp
1	pound cooked pasta	1	can artichoke hearts, drained
3/4	stick butter	2	cloves garlic, chopped
1	pound sliced mushrooms	1/2	pound jumbo lump crabmeat
1	medium onion, sliced	1	lemon, juiced
			salt and pepper, to taste

In a medium sauce pan sauté onions, garlic, salt and pepper in butter over medium to high heat until translucent (about 2 to 4 minutes), add mushrooms and sauté about 2 more minutes. Add shrimp sauté 2 more minutes add artichoke hearts, crabmeat and lemon juice, sauté about 2 more minutes or until heated through. Add salt and pepper, to taste.

• • • • • • • • • • • • • • •

Lay a bed of pasta on a plate, place fish over pasta and top with sauté mixture and enjoy!

Main Dishes

Eggplant, Shrimp and Crabmeat

4	long skinny eggplant	1	egg
1	cup chopped onion	2	cups Italian bread crumbs
1	cup chopped green onion	1	pound crabmeat
½	cup chopped parsley	1	pound shrimp
½	cup chopped celery		olive oil
1	garlic clove		butter

Boil eggplant in salted water until tender. Drain and keep stock. In olive oil, sauté onions, garlic, celery and parsley until clear. Add shrimp and cook until they turn pink. Remove from heat and add eggplant, 1 cup bread crumbs, egg, and a little stock. Blend in crabmeat. Pour into casserole dish and top with remaining bread crumbs. Drizzle with butter. Bake at 350° for about 30 minutes.

Blend of Bayou Casserole

1	cup rice, cooked	2	stalks celery, chopped
1	stick margarine	2	tablespoons margarine
1	8-ounce package cream cheese	1	can mushrooms
1	pound peeled shrimp	1	10¾-ounce can cream of mushroom soup
1	pint crabmeat or crawfish tails		
1	large onion, chopped	½	teaspoon hot sauce
1	bell pepper, chopped	1	tablespoon garlic salt
2	cups grated sharp Cheddar cheese		dash red pepper

Melt stick of margarine and cream cheese in a bowl in microwave. Sauté shrimp, crabmeat or crawfish tails, onion, green pepper and celery in 2 tablespoons margarine. Add remaining ingredients (including margarine/cream cheese mixture) except Cheddar cheese. Mix well. Pour into 9x13-inch casserole dish. Top with Cheddar cheese.

Bake at 350° for 30 to 45 minutes or until bubbly. Hot sauce and red pepper according to your own preference.

Main Dishes

Crawfish Étouffée

1	cup uncooked rice	1	green bell pepper, chopped
10	tablespoons unsalted butter, divided	4	celery stalks, chopped
		5	garlic cloves, minced
1	pound frozen cooked and peeled crawfish tails, thawed and drained	6	tablespoons all-purpose flour
		2¾	cups chicken broth
		¼	cup chopped green onions
1	medium yellow onion, chopped	1	tablespoon Cajun seasoning

Cook rice according to package. Melt 4 tablespoons butter in a large pot over medium-high heat; add crawfish, and cook 5 minutes or until thoroughly heated. Remove crawfish, and keep warm. Add onion, bell pepper, and celery to pot. Cook over medium-high heat until tender. Add garlic, and cook 1 minute. Remove vegetables, and keep warm. Melt remaining 6 tablespoons butter in pot over medium heat. Add flour, and cook, stirring constantly with a wire whisk, until caramel colored. Reduce heat to low, and gradually stir in chicken broth and next 5 ingredients. Cook over medium heat until thickened. Stir in vegetables and crawfish; cook 5 minutes. Serve with rice.

6 SERVINGS.

Pass Christian Crabmeat Casserole

1	pound fresh lump crabmeat	1	14-ounce package shredded Cheddar cheese
1	14-ounce package cream cheese, cubed	¼	cup milk
		2	ounces cooking sherry

Mix all the ingredients and put into a 2-quart glass casserole dish Bake at 350° for about 35 minutes.

4 TO 6 SERVINGS.

Main Dishes

Linguine with Shrimp Scampi

	vegetable oil	2	pounds shrimp, peeled and deveined
	salt		
1½	pounds linguine	½	teaspoon black pepper
6	tablespoons unsalted butter		grated zest of 1 lemon
5	tablespoons olive oil	½	cup freshly squeezed lemon juice
10	cloves garlic, minced	¼	teaspoon red pepper flakes

Drizzle some oil in a large pot of boiling salted water and cook the linguine according to the directions on the package. In a large pan, melt the butter and olive oil over medium-low heat. Add the garlic. Sauté for 1 minute. Add the shrimp, 1 teaspoon of salt, and the pepper and sauté until the shrimp have just turned pink. Remove from the heat; add the lemon zest, lemon juice, and red pepper flakes. Toss to combine. Drain the linguine and place back in the pot. Toss with the shrimp and sauce.

Louisiana Crawfish Dressing

6	cups sliced squash	1	teaspoon creole seasoning
2	cups water	1	pound crawfish tails, peeled
1	large onion, chopped	½	teaspoon salt
1	green bell pepper, chopped	¼	teaspoon pepper
1	cup celery, chopped	¼	teaspoon dried whole thyme
½	cup melted butter	⅛	teaspoon red pepper
1	egg, slightly beaten	⅛	teaspoon hot sauce
⅓	cup grated Parmesan cheese		

Combine squash and water in Dutch oven; cook until tender, drain well. Sauté onion and next 2 ingredients in butter until tender. Add vegetable mixture and egg to squash. Stir in remaining ingredients. Spoon mixture into a greased 12x8x2-inch baking dish. Bake at 350° for 30 minutes.

Main Dishes

Chalu Pa

1	pound pinto beans, dried	4	pounds pork roast
7	cups water	½	cup chopped onions
2	garlic cloves, minced	2	tablespoons chili powder
2	tablespoons salt	1	teaspoon oregano
1	tablespoon cumin	1	can chopped green chilies

Place all ingredients in a large pot. Cook until roast is tender, about 2½ to 3 hours. Remove roast, chop and shred and return to pot. Simmer an additional 30 to 45 minutes.

Garnish

chopped green onions	sour cream
chopped tomato	avocado
shredded cheese	cilantro
chopped black olives	

May serve in flour tortilla or over corn chips.

Ginger Glazed Pork Tenderloin

1	2-pound pork tenderloin	1	tablespoon water
½	teaspoon salt	1	tablespoon soy sauce
⅓	cup apricot preserves	1	tablespoon grated fresh ginger
3	garlic cloves, minced		(or 1 teaspoon ground ginger)

Place pork tenderloin on a lightly greased rack in a foil-lined roasting pan. Sprinkle evenly with salt. Combine preserves and next 4 ingredients. Spread evenly over pork. Bake at 425° for 25 minutes. Remove from oven; cover and let stand 10 minutes.

Main Dishes

Dry Rubbed Barbecue Ribs with Dipping Sauce

2-3 pound slab of pork ribs

Rub

½ cup paprika	½ cup brown sugar
¼ cup black pepper	2 tablespoons chili powder
½ cup garlic salt	2 tablespoons oregano

Basting Spray

1 cup apple cider vinegar	1 cup white wine
¼ cup balsamic vinegar	

Put a generous amount of rub on ribs, massaging it into the meaty side of the rib, put them on an oiled grill rack in a smoker for 4 hours at 165°. Baste ribs once or twice an hour with basting spray. When meat has pulled away from the bone about ½-inch the ribs are ready.

Sauce for Dipping

2 cups ketchup	2 tablespoons prepared mustard
¼ cup apple cider vinegar	1 tablespoon hot sauce
¼ cup Worcestershire sauce	1 tablespoon barbecue rub
¼ cup firmly packed brown sugar	2 teaspoons liquid smoke
2 tablespoons molasses	1 teaspoon black pepper

Combine all ingredients in a saucepan and bring slowly to a boil over medium-high heat. Reduce the heat to medium and gently simmer the sauce until dark, thick, and richly flavored, 10 to 15 minutes. The sauce can be transferred to a jar to be stored in the refrigerator, and will keep for several months.

Main Dishes

Herbed Pork Medallions

1½ pounds pork tenderloin	½ teaspoon dried thyme
2 tablespoons butter or margarine, melted	½ teaspoon paprika
¼ teaspoon garlic powder	⅛ teaspoon pepper
½ teaspoon salt	⅛ teaspoon red pepper
½ teaspoon dried tarragon	1 tablespoon honey

Cut pork into ½ in slices and pound to flatten. Combine butter and garlic powder; brush over pork. Combine the seasonings; sprinkle over pork. Place in 2 greased 15x10x1-inch baking pans. Broil 4 to 6 inches from the heat for 5 minutes; turn and broil 3 minutes longer. Brush with honey; broil for 1 minute or until meat juices run clear.

6 SERVINGS.

Marinated Pork Tenderloin

1 5½-ounce can apricot nectar	2 teaspoons minced fresh parsley
2 garlic cloves, minced	3 tablespoons vegetable oil
½ cup soy sauce	2 1-pound pork tenderloins

In a large resealable bag, combine the first 5 ingredients. Add the pork; seal bag and turn to coat. Refrigerate for at least 2 hours. Drain and discard the marinade. Line a shallow baking pan with foil and coat with nonstick cooking spray. Place tenderloins in pan. Bake, uncovered at 425° for 25 to 30 minutes or until a meat thermometer reads 160°. Let stand for 10 minutes before slicing.

6 SERVINGS.

Main Dishes

Pork Chop Casserole

6 pork chops
3 thinly sliced potatoes
1 thinly sliced onion

1 11-ounce can cream of mushroom soup
1 cup Cheddar cheese

Preheat oven to 350°. Brown pork chops in skillet. Layer onions and potatoes in dish. Place pork chops on top. Pour soup over the mixture and add cheese. Bake for 30 minutes.

Pork Chops with Spices

4 pork chops
garlic salt or garlic powder
onion salt or onion powder
lemon pepper

Greek seasoning
Creole seasoning, optional
2 tablespoons butter
2 chicken or beef bouillon cubes

Melt butter in a skillet. Season the pork chops. Brown the pork chops on each side. Reduce the heat. Dissolve the bouillon cubes in 3/4 cup of water. Add this to the skillet. Cover and cook until the pork chops are done.

Pork Tenderloin

2/3 cup soy sauce
1/3 cup oil
2 tablespoons Karo syrup

2 teaspoons dry mustard
2 teaspoons ground ginger
2 garlic cloves, minced

Marinate pork overnight in this mixture overnight and grill for 20 to 30 minutes. Baste the meat with the marinade constantly.

Main Dishes

Roasted Rosemary Pork Loin

	cooking spray	2	teaspoons salt
4	pound boneless pork loin	½	teaspoon black pepper
2	tablespoons spicy mustard	2	tablespoons chopped fresh
2	cloves garlic, minced		rosemary leaves
2	tablespoons chopped red onion		

Preheat oven to 350°. Spray a shallow roasting pan with cooking spray and set aside. Trim any excess fat from the pork loin, leaving a wide, thin strip of fat running down the center of the top. Rub the entire pork loin evenly with the mustard, followed by the garlic, red onion, salt and pepper. Make sure to really rub in the spices. Sprinkle the rosemary evenly over the top. Place the pork loin in the roasting pan and bake for 20 minutes. Reduce the heat to 300° and continue baking for about 1 hour, until it registers 145° in the thickest part of the loin. Let the loin rest for about 10 minutes before slicing.

Southwestern Pull-Apart Ring

1	12-ounce package ground hot pork sausage	2	12-ounce cans refrigerated biscuits
1	red bell pepper, diced	1½	cups shredded Mexican cheese
1	green bell pepper, diced		blend
1	1-ounce package fajita seasoning mix		

Cook sausage in a skillet over medium heat, stirring until it crumbles and is no longer pink. Stir in peppers and cook 3 to 5 minutes or until tender. Sprinkle with seasoning mix and cook 1 to 2 more minutes; drain well, pressing with paper towels. Separate refrigerated biscuits, and cut into quarters; place in a large mixing bowl. Fold in sausage mixture, tossing to coat. Layer biscuit mixture and cheese in a lightly greased 10-inch tube pan. Bake at 400° for 15 minutes or until golden brown. Let stand in pan for 5 to 10 minutes. Invert onto a serving plate and serve immediately.

Main Dishes

Quick Pork Chops

5	thinly sliced pork chops	2	eggs, slightly beaten
2	cups Italian bread crumbs	1/4	cup milk

Wash and rinse pork chops, set aside. In a medium mixing bowl beat eggs and milk together, set aside, Pour bread crumbs on wax paper. Dip pork chops in egg mixture and coat with bread crumbs. Fry in hot oil until golden brown.

Eggplant Eugene

1	medium eggplant, sliced and peeled	1	egg, beaten
1/2	cup plain flour	1	cup tomato sauce
3	tablespoons oil	1	tablespoon oregano
		3/4	cup Parmesan cheese

In a mixing bowl, dip each slice of eggplant in beaten egg. Place in flour and coat well. Fry in oil until brown and drain. In a baking dish, layer 1/2 of eggplant pieces, 1/2 of tomato sauce and oregano. Repeat layers and top with Parmesan Cheese. Bake for 30 minutes at 350° in an 8x8-inch baking dish.

4 SERVINGS.

Easter Ham

1	3- to 4-pound fully cooked spiral sliced ham	1 1/2	cups apricot preserves
		3	tablespoons prepared mustard

Preheat oven to 350°. Place ham in aluminum foil lined pan. In a bowl combine preserves and mustard. Pour over ham. Bake for 1 1/2 hours. Baste every 30 minutes with glaze.

Main Dishes

Country Meat Loaf

1	large egg, beaten	1½	pounds ground chuck
1	tablespoon salt	½	cup finely chopped celery
½	cup soft bread crumbs	½	cup ketchup
½	teaspoon pepper	¼	cup finely chopped fresh
½	cup finely chopped onion		mushrooms
1	clove garlic, minced	1	tablespoon water
½	cup finely chopped green pepper		

Combine first 9 ingredients in a large bowl. Add ground chuck and stir until just blended. Shape into an 8x4-inch freeform loaf on a greased rack of a broiler pan. Bake at 350° for 30 minutes. Combine ketchup and water and spoon over loaf. Bake 45 more minutes or until done.

6 SERVINGS.

Turkey Meat Loaf

3	cups chopped onion	1½	teaspoons tomato paste
2	tablespoons olive oil	2	pounds ground turkey breast
2	teaspoons salt	1½	cups Italian bread crumbs
2	teaspoons black pepper	2	large eggs beaten
⅓	cup Worcestershire sauce	¾	cup ketchup
½	cup chicken stock		

Preheat the oven to 325°. In a medium pan, on medium-low heat, cook the onions, olive oil, salt, and pepper until the onions are translucent. Add the Worcestershire sauce, chicken stock, and tomato paste and mix well. Allow to cool to room temperature. Combine the turkey, bread crumbs, eggs, and onion mixture in a large bowl. Mix well and place into a loaf pan. Spread the ketchup evenly on top. Bake for 1½ hours or until the internal temperature is 160° and the meat loaf is cooked through.

Main Dishes

Stuffed Turkey (or Chicken) Breasts

1	pound skinless, boneless, turkey breasts	2	tablespoons oil-packed sun-dried tomatoes, drained and chopped
4	teaspoons oil from sun-dried tomatoes, divided	2	tablespoons prepared pesto sauce, divided
¼	cup chopped onion	4	tablespoons grated Parmesan cheese
½	cup seasoned bread crumbs		
¼	cup low salt chicken broth	1	package spaghetti, cooked and drained

Pat turkey breasts dry. Pound flat. In a large nonstick skillet, over medium-high heat, heat 2 teaspoons tomato oil. Add onion and sauté 2 minutes, or until wilted. Remove from heat. To the same skillet, add bread crumbs, chicken broth, sun-dried tomatoes and 1 tablespoon pesto; toss lightly. Put mixture on middle of turkey breast; secure with a toothpick or string. In the same skillet, over medium-high heat, heat remaining 2 teaspoons tomato oil. Brown turkey breasts in hot oil 3 minutes on each side. Reduce heat to medium, cover skillet and cook 6 minutes. Turn breasts over and brush with remaining 1 tablespoon pesto. Cover and cook through. Sprinkle with Parmesan cheese; slice and serve over spaghetti.

Mexican Casserole

1	large can tamales	½	cup diced onions
1½	cups cooked rice	1	bag shredded Cheddar cheese
2	cans chili, no beans	1	small can black olives, optional

In a 9x13-inch dish, slice or crush tamales. Add cooked rice over tamales. Spread chili over rice. Next add onions and top with shredded cheese. Drain and slice black olives and dot on top of dish. Cook 30 to 45 minutes in 350° oven or until cheese is bubbly, hot and slightly browned.

Main Dishes

Turkey Pot Pie

3	tablespoons unsalted butter
2	medium leeks, white and tender green parts only, thinly sliced
2	large carrots, diced
2	celery stalks, thinly sliced
½	pound button mushrooms, quartered
½	pound shiitake mushrooms, stemmed and sliced
1½	cups turkey or chicken stock

3	tablespoons unbleached all-purpose flour
2	cups cooked turkey meat, cut into bite-size pieces
½	cup heavy cream
1½	teaspoons dried thyme
1	9-inch pie crust
1	prepared pie top salt and pepper, to taste

Preheat oven to 400°. Melt 2 tablespoons butter in a large heavy skillet. Add the leeks, carrots, and celery and cook over medium heat until softened but not browned, about 10 minutes. Set aside. Add remaining butter to skillet and sauté mushrooms over medium high heat until they have given off their moisture and are tender, about 10 minutes. Combine with leek mixture in skillet. Over medium high heat, stir the flour into skillet and cook for 1 minute. Add the stock slowly, while stirring, and bring to simmer. Stir until nicely thickened. Add the turkey, cream and thyme and season with salt and pepper. With a slotted spoon, fill pie crust with filling. Pour in any remaining liquid until crust is almost filled to the top. Moisten edge of pie crust with water and place pie top on top, sealing the edges with a fork. Cut slits into the top of the pie. Bake for 30 to 40 minutes until pie crust is golden brown and filling is bubbling.

6 SERVINGS.

Italian Cheese and Tomato Pizza

1	pound frozen pizza dough, thawed	2	large tomatoes
¼	cup shredded Parmesan cheese	2	cups fresh grated mozzarella cheese
⅛	cup olive oil	¼	cup shredded fresh basil leaves

Preheat oven to 425°. On a lightly floured surface, roll dough into a 14-inch circle and place on a greased baking sheet. Top the dough with olive oil, mozzarella, Parmesan cheese and sliced tomatoes. Place pizza in oven; bake 5 to 7 minutes or until crust is golden and cheese is melted. Remove from oven and let rest 5 minutes. Sprinkle with basil.

Spinach Quiche

1	unbaked 10-inch pie crust	1	13½-ounce can spinach, well drained
½	cup grated Cheddar or Gruyère cheese	¼	cup bacon bits
4	eggs, beaten	1	Roma tomato, thinly sliced
1	cup reduced fat milk		

Preheat oven 425°. Prepare crust according to package directions. Sprinkle cheese on pie crust. Mix eggs, milk, spinach, and bacon bits; pour mixture evenly over cheese. Top with tomato slices. Bake 15 minutes, reduce heat to 350° and bake an additional 20 to 25 minutes until set, or a toothpick inserted in center comes out clean. Remove from oven and let stand 10 minutes.

4 SERVINGS.

• • • • • • • • • • • • • •

Vegetarian Quiche: *substitute ⅓ cup diced red onion in place of bacon bits.*

Main Dishes

Sausage and Cheese Quiche

3 tablespoons cornstarch	2 cups grated Cheddar cheese
3 large eggs	1 cup ground hot sausage
1 cup mayonnaise	1 frozen deep dish pie shell
1 cup chopped green onions	

Cook sausage. Drain and chop into small pieces. Mix all other ingredients well. Add sausage. For best taste results, mix all ingredients and store overnight in sealed container in refrigerator. Next morning, pour into pie shell and bake approximately 1 hour in a 350° oven, or until well done. Cool about 10 minutes before slicing.

Savory Cheddar Egg Bake

4 slices each wheat, rye and Italian bread, cut into 1-inch cubes	½ teaspoon dried minced onion
2 cups fully cooked ham	½ teaspoon dried basil
2 cups shredded Cheddar cheese, divided	⅛ teaspoon pepper
1 teaspoon minced fresh parsley	6 eggs
	2½ cups milk

Layer half of the bread cubes in a greased 13x9-inch baking dish. Sprinkle with ham and 1 cup cheese. Top with remaining bread cubes. Combine the parsley, onion, basil and pepper; sprinkle over the bread. In a bowl, beat the eggs and milk; pour over the top. Sprinkle with the remaining cheese. Cover and refrigerate over night. Remove from refrigerator 30 minutes before baking. Bake, uncovered, at 350° for 40 to 50 minutes or until a knife inserted near the center comes out clean.

8 SERVINGS.

Main Dishes

Sausage and Mushroom Quiche

½	pound bulk sausage	1	tablespoon lemon juice
¾	pound thinly sliced mushrooms	½	teaspoon salt
4	tablespoons butter	¼	teaspoon pepper
1	cup heavy cream	1	10-inch pastry shell, partially cooked
1	tablespoon flour		
2	egg yolks, slightly beaten	½	cup Parmesan cheese
1	tablespoon butter, melted		

Preheat oven to 350°. Brown sausage, breaking it up with fork. Drain well. Sauté mushrooms in butter. Mix cream, egg yolks, flour, butter, lemon juice, salt and pepper. Put sausage and mushrooms in pie shell, pour custard over, sprinkle with cheese; bake 35 minutes until puffy and light brown.

Spinach Stuffed Manicotti

1	10-ounce package frozen chopped spinach, thawed	1	cup ricotta cheese
		8	dried manicotti shells, cooked
1	teaspoon dried Italian seasoning	1	cup shredded mozzarella cheese
½	8-ounce package cream cheese, softened	2	cups pasta sauce
¼	teaspoon salt	1	cup freshly grated Parmesan cheese, divided

Press spinach between layers of paper towels to remove excess moisture. Combine spinach, cream cheese, ricotta cheese, mozzarella cheese, ½ cup Parmesan cheese, Italian seasoning and salt, stirring well. Stuff mixture evenly into manicotti shells. Pour ½ cup pasta sauce into a lightly greased 11x7-inch baking dish. Arrange stuffed shells over sauce. Spoon remaining 1½ cups pasta sauce over shells. Cover and bake at 350° for 30 minutes or until thoroughly heated. Sprinkle with remaining ½ cup Parmesan cheese; bake, uncovered for 5 more minutes or until cheese melts.

4 SERVINGS.

Main Dishes

Spinach and Cheese Filled Shell Noodles

2	10-ounce packages chopped frozen spinach, thawed and drained	¼	teaspoon ground nutmeg
½	cup shredded Swiss cheese	¼	cup flour
½	cup freshly grated Parmesan cheese	1¾	cups milk
⅓	butter	1	jar spaghetti sauce
½	teaspoon salt		shredded Swiss cheese for topping
¼	teaspoon pepper	1	box large shell noodles (can use manicotti noodles also)

Squeeze thawed spinach as dry as possible. Melt butter, stir in flour, salt, pepper and nutmeg. Stir continuously. Cook until it bubbles for 1 minute. Stir in milk; cook and stir until thickened and bubbles for 2 minutes. Stir in spinach and cheeses. Stir until cheese melts. Pour a little spaghetti sauce into the bottom of a 13x9-inch pan. Fill large shell noodles with spinach mixture. Place shells open side down in pan. Pour remaining spaghetti sauce over shells, sprinkle with Swiss cheese. Bake covered at 350° for 30 to 45 minutes, last 10 to 15 minutes bake uncovered. Baking is just to warm thoroughly.

• • • • • • • • • • • • • •

If you make and bake them the same day you can reduce the baking time to probably 20 minutes or until warmed completely. Freezes well.

Sicilian Spaghetti Sauce

2 tablespoons extra-virgin olive oil
4 garlic cloves, or to taste
1 teaspoon basil, or to taste
1 teaspoon oregano, or to taste

1 6-ounce can tomato paste
3 8-ounce cans tomato sauce
3 8-ounce cans water

Meatballs

1 pound ground chuck
Italian seasoning, to taste

salt and pepper, to taste

In a black iron skillet sauté garlic in 2 tablespoons olive oil over very low heat for approximately 2 minutes. Add basil and oregano and continue to sauté for 5 minutes. Add tomato paste and mix thoroughly. Continue cooking for 3 minutes. Add 1 can of tomato sauce. Mix well and cook 3 to 4 minutes. Add 2nd can of tomato sauce. Mix well and cook 3-4 minutes. Add 3rd can of tomato sauce. Mix well and cook 3 to 4 minutes. Add 1 (8-ounce) can of water. Mix well. Cook at a low temperature for 5 minutes. Add the 2nd and 3rd can of water at 5 minute intervals, mixing well. Cook, on low, for 2 hours. Add meatballs. Cook additional hour (or longer). Serve over spaghetti.

Gyro Roast

1	3½-pound leg of lamb, boned
2½	pounds boneless beef round steak
¼	cup dried oregano leaves
2	teaspoons dried dill weed
3	teaspoons garlic powder
½	teaspoon ground thyme
1½	teaspoons salt
1	teaspoon pepper
	olive oil

Pound lamb and beef on both sides with meat mallet, until each piece measures 12x14 inches. Combine herbs, salt and pepper, crushing with back of spoon until fine in texture, but not powdered. Place lamb on cutting board; brush top lightly with oil and sprinkle with ⅓ herb mixture. Pound herbs into surface of lamb with meat mallet. Lay round steak on top of lamb; brush top lightly with olive oil and sprinkle with ½ remaining herb mixture. Pound herbs into surface of beef with meat mallet. Roll up meats as tightly as possible, starting at short end. Tie securely in several places with a string. Brush outside of roast lightly with oil; rub remaining herb mixture into surface of meat. Place roast in center of the cooking grate and cook until internal temperature registers 140°, about 1½ hours, turning roast every 45 minutes. Outside of meat will become very dark and crusty. Remove meat from cooking grate and let stand 15 minutes before slicing. Slice thinly.

Notes

Notes

Vegetalbes & Side Dishes

Cabbage, Casseroles,
Green Beans, Grits,
Broccoli, Potatoes,
Corn, Asparagus, etc.

Apple Walnut Cabbage

6 slices bacon	½ medium cabbage, shredded
½ cup firmly packed light brown sugar	½ medium-size red cabbage, shredded
½ cup water	2 medium cooking apples, thinly sliced with peel on
⅓ cup cider vinegar	½ cup chopped walnuts, toasted

Cook bacon in a large Dutch oven medium heat until crisp; remove bacon reserving 3 tablespoons drippings in pan. Crumble bacon and set aside. Add sugar, water, and vinegar to drippings; cook over medium-high heat 3 to 4 minutes or until liquid is reduced to ¾ cup. Add cabbage; cook, stirring constantly, 4 minutes or until cabbage wilts. Add apples; toss gently. Remove from heat. Sprinkle with bacon and walnuts. Serve immediately.

6 SERVINGS.

Artichoke Casserole

1 12½-ounce can artichoke hearts, reserve liquid	2 garlic cloves, minced
⅓ cup Italian bread crumbs	1 teaspoon minced onions
	½ cup olive oil

Drain hearts, reserve liquid and thinly slice. Combine all other ingredients, including liquid. Begin layering artichoke hearts and crumb mixture ending with bread crumbs. Bake at 325° for 20 minutes.

Vegetables & Side Dishes

Artichoke Au Gratin

5	tablespoons butter divided	4	ounces Cheddar cheese
3	tablespoons all-purpose flour	½	cup mayonnaise
½	teaspoon salt		black pepper, to taste
1¾	cups milk	¼	cup fine dry bread crumbs
2	14-ounce cans artichokes hearts, rinsed, drained and chopped		

Preheat oven to 325°. In a 2-quart saucepan, melt 3 tablespoons butter. Add flour and salt. Stir until smooth. Cook and stir for 1 minute. Gradually add the milk. Cook over medium heat, stirring constantly until thickened and bubbly. Remove from heat. Stir in artichoke hearts, cheese, mayonnaise, and pepper. Spoon into a 1½-quart casserole.

Melt the remaining 2 tablespoons butter. Stir in bread crumbs and sprinkle over top. Bake about 45 minutes.

6 SERVINGS.

Asparagus Casserole

1	12-ounce can asparagus, drained		salt and pepper, to taste
2	ounces butter, melted	1	cup crushed buttery round crackers
4	ounces cubed Cheddar cheese		
1	cup milk		

Combine asparagus and butter in a 2-quart baking dish, and top with cheese. Whisk together milk, and pour over cheese. Season with salt and pepper, to taste, and sprinkle with cracker crumbs. Bake at 350° for 45 minutes.

Vegetables & Side Dishes

Aunt Jean's Squash Casserole

2	pounds squash	½	cup milk
2	eggs	1	teaspoon salt
1	small onion, chopped	2	cups shredded Cheddar cheese
6	teaspoons margarine		crushed butter crackers
3	teaspoons brown sugar		butter or margarine

Cut squash into rounds and cook in small amount of water (approximately 2 cups) until tender. Drain well and mash. In a separate bowl, beat eggs. Sauté onion in margarine. Add squash, eggs, milk, brown sugar and salt to onions. Mix well. In a buttered 2-quart casserole, put 1 layer of 10 crushed crackers, 1 layer of squash mixture and 1 layer of cheese. Repeat the 3 layers; top with cracker crumbs and dot with butter. Bake uncovered at 350° for 45 minutes.

8 TO 10 SERVINGS.

• • • • • • • • • • • • • • •

Can be frozen.

Breakfast Casserole

1	24-ounce package frozen shredded potatoes	1	12-ounce container cottage cheese
12	eggs, beaten		dash hot sauce
1	8-ounce package shredded cheese		dash paprika
4	chopped green onions		salt and pepper, to taste

Spray 13x9-inch pan with cooking spray. Crumble potatoes in pan, uncooked. Combine all other ingredients except paprika. Pour over potatoes. Sprinkle with paprika. Bake 50 to 60 minutes at 350° uncovered. Let stand 10 minutes. May be made low-fat using egg substitute and low-fat cheeses.

8 SERVINGS.

Vegetables & Side Dishes

Breakfast in One Dish

2   cups water
½   teaspoon salt
½   cup uncooked grits
4   cups shredded Cheddar cheese
7   eggs, beaten (add more if
       necessary)

1   cup milk
      garlic salt, to taste
2   pounds sausage, cooked,
       crumbled and drained

Bring water and salt to boil; stir in grits. Return to a boil; reduce heat. Cook 4 minutes, stirring occasionally. Combine grits and cheese in large bowl; stir until cheese is melted. Combine eggs, milk, and garlic salt; mix well. Add small amount of hot grits mixture to egg mixture, stirring well. Stir egg mixture into remaining grit mixture. Add cooked sausage; mix well. Pour into greased Pyrex baking dish. Cover and refrigerate overnight. Remove from refrigerator and let stand 15 minutes. Bake at 350° for 50 minutes.

• • • • • • • • • • • • • • •

Freezes well

Broccoli Casserole

2   10-ounce packages frozen
       broccoli spears
½   cup mayonnaise
1   cup shredded Cheddar cheese
½   cup finely chopped onion
2   large eggs, beaten

¾   cup herbed-seasoned stuffing
       mix
1   10¾-ounce can cream of
       mushroom soup, undiluted
2   tablespoons butter or
       margarine, melted

Cook broccoli according to package directions and drain. Arrange broccoli in a lightly greased 11x7-inch baking dish. Sprinkle with cheese. Combine eggs and next 3 ingredients; spread over cheese. Combine stuffing mix and butter; sprinkle over casserole. Bake at 350° for 30 minutes or until thoroughly heated.

Vegetables & Side Dishes

Breakfast Potato Casserole

2   pounds frozen hash browns, thawed
½   cup margarine
1   teaspoon salt
1   teaspoon pepper

1   10¾-ounce can cream of chicken soup
½   cup chopped onion
1   pint sour cream
1   10-ounce package grated sharp Cheddar cheese

Topping

2   cups crushed corn flakes

½   cup melted margarine

Mix all ingredients (except for topping) and pour in buttered casserole dish. Cover with corn flakes and drizzle melted margarine over entire casserole. Bake 350° oven for at least 1 hour.

12 TO 15 SERVINGS.

Broccoli Cornbread

1   box cornbread mix
1   stick butter
1   small onion, chopped

1   box frozen broccoli thawed and drained
4   eggs slightly beaten
1   6-ounce container cottage cheese

Preheat oven 400°. Melt butter in 8x8-inch pan. Mix chopped onions and broccoli and add remaining ingredients. Pour into pan with butter. Bake for 30 to 45 minutes or until cornbread is brown.

Broccoli Rice Casserole

1   10-ounce package frozen
    chopped broccoli
1   8-ounce jar pasteurized process
    cheese sauce
1   8-ounce package processed hot
    Mexican cheese
½   stick margarine

1   small onion, chopped
1   bell pepper, chopped
¾   cup uncooked rice
1   10¾-ounce can cream of
    mushroom soup
1   11-ounce can cream of chicken
    soup

Cook rice per package directions. Cook broccoli. Sauté onion and bell pepper
in margarine. Combine all ingredients in greased casserole dish. Bake 25 to
30 minutes at 350°.

Cabbage Rolls

1   large cabbage
1   pound ground beef
1   pound sausage
1   small onion
1½ cups prepared rice
2   eggs, beaten

1   8-ounce can tomato sauce
1   can tomato soup
1   bay leaf
    salt and pepper
    brown sugar

Steam cabbage until tender. Pull off leaves and set aside. Combine ground
beef, sausage, rice, eggs, onion, 1 teaspoon salt, ½ teaspoon pepper in a large
bowl. Fill each leaf with a large spoonful of mixture. Wrap leaf around mixture
and place in a Dutch oven or deep 9x13-inch pan. Mix soup with ½ can water.
Pour over cabbage rolls. Pour tomato sauce over top of soup. Sprinkle with
brown sugar. Add a bay leaf. Cover with foil. Bake for 1 hour at 300°. Uncover
and bake an additional 30 minutes.

Vegetables & Side Dishes

Cajun Green Beans

6   slices of cooked bacon, crumbled
    with drippings reserved
½   cup green peppers chopped
¼   cup onion, chopped
2   tablespoons all-purpose flour
2   tablespoons brown sugar
1   tablespoon Worcestershire
    sauce

½   teaspoon salt
¼   teaspoon pepper
⅛   teaspoon dry mustard
1   16-ounce can peeled whole
    tomatoes, cut into fourths
1   16-ounce can green beans,
    drained

In a skillet with bacon drippings, sauté green pepper and onion until tender. Blend together next 6 ingredients and stir into skillet. Add tomatoes and continue to stir until mixture thickens. Add green beans and heat thoroughly. Sprinkle with crumbed bacon.

6 SERVINGS.

Cheesy Grits

2   cups quick grits
4   ounces unsalted butter
1½ cups grated sharp Cheddar
    cheese

2   tablespoons sea salt
1½ teaspoons hot sauce
½   teaspoon garlic powder
½   cup Parmesan cheese

Cook grits until done. Let grits sit for 10 minutes. Add butter, cheese, salt, hot sauce, garlic powder, and Parmesan cheese. Whisk grits until cheese is melted and consistency is uniform.

Classic Sweet Potato Casserole

Topping

1	cup brown sugar	⅓	cup butter, melted
½	cup all-purpose flour	1	cup chopped pecans

Casserole

3	cups cooked sweet potatoes, peeled	2	eggs
½	cup sugar	⅓	cup milk
½	cup butter, softened	1	teaspoon vanilla extract

Preheat oven to 350°. In a small bowl, combine the topping ingredients. Set aside.

In a large bowl, mash the cooked sweet potatoes. Add the ½ cup butter, eggs, milk, and vanilla extract. Beat with electric mixer on medium speed until well blended. Place mixture in a greased 9x13-inch baking dish. Crumble topping over mixture. Bake for 30 minutes.

8 SERVINGS.

Company Carrots

1	16-ounce package baby carrots	¾	cup water
1	cup apple juice	⅓	cup honey

In a large saucepan, combine all ingredients. Bring to a boil. Reduce heat; cover and simmer for 10 minutes or until carrots are tender.

4 SERVINGS.

Vegetables & Side Dishes

Cornbread Dressing

2	6-ounce packages cornbread mix	1	teaspoon salt
½	cup butter	4½	cups chicken broth
2	cups chopped onions	1	11-ounce can cream of chicken
2	cups chopped celery		soup
2	cups crumbled biscuits	3	eggs, beaten
1	tablespoon poultry seasoning		

Prepare, and bake cornbread mix according to the package directions. Cool, crumble and set aside. Preheat oven to 350°. In a large skillet over medium high heat on stove top, melt butter. Add onion and celery; cook, stirring constantly, until tender. In a large bowl, combine crumbled cornbread, crumbled biscuits, poultry seasoning and salt; stir in onions and celery. Add broth, soup and eggs, stirring well. Pour mixture into a lightly greased 9x13x2-inch baking dish. Bake for 50 minutes or until center is set.

Crab Casserole

1	can crabmeat	1½	cups milk
½	teaspoon salt	½	cup melted butter
5	slices white bread	2	hard-boiled eggs
	dash of pepper	¼	pound Cheddar cheese, cubed

Preheat oven to 350°. Break bread into small pieces and soak in milk for 10 minutes. Add crabmeat, eggs, cheese, seasonings, and butter. Mix well. Place in casserole dish, cover and bake for 45 minutes.

4 TO 6 SERVINGS.

Vegetables & Side Dishes

Cranberry Sauce

1½ cups sugar
1 naval orange
½ teaspoon grated ginger

4 cups cranberries, rinsed and drained
½ cup toasted pecans

Grate orange peel and add to a pot with the sugar and ginger. Add the juice of the orange into the pot and simmer over medium heat until the sugar is dissolved. Add the cranberries and cook until they pop (approximately 5 minutes). Add the pecans and cool sauce.

Creamy Christmas Cauliflower

1 large head cauliflower, broken into florets
2 cups milk
¼ cup diced green pepper
1 cup shredded Swiss cheese
1 7.3-ounce jar sliced mushrooms, drained

2 tablespoons diced pimientos
¼ cup butter
1 teaspoon salt
⅓ cup all-purpose flour
paprika, optional

In a large saucepan, cook cauliflower in a small amount of water for 6 to 7 minutes or until crisp-tender; drain well. In a medium saucepan, sauté green peppers and mushrooms in butter for 2 minutes. Add Flour; gradually stir in milk. Bring to a boil; boil for 2 minutes, stirring constantly. Remove from heat; stir in cheese until melted. Add pimientos and salt. Place half of the cauliflower in a greased 2-quart baking dish; top with half of the sauce. Repeat layers. Bake uncovered at 325° for 25 minutes or until bubbly. Sprinkle with paprika if desired.

8 TO 10 SERVINGS.

Vegetables & Side Dishes

Eleanor's Macaroni and Cheese

2 cups cottage cheese
1 8-ounce container sour cream
1 large egg
³/₄ teaspoon salt
¹/₂ teaspoon pepper

2 cups shredded sharp Cheddar cheese
1 8-ounce package macaroni, cooked
paprika

Stir together first 6 ingredients in a large bowl; stir in macaroni. Spoon mixture into a lightly greased 2-quart baking dish and sprinkle with paprika. Bake at 350° for 45 minutes. Let stand 10 to 15 minutes prior to serving.

Garlic Butter and Cashew Broccoli

1¹/₂ pounds fresh broccoli
¹/₂ cup butter or margarine
1 tablespoon brown sugar
3 tablespoons soy sauce

2 teaspoons white vinegar
¹/₄ teaspoon pepper
¹/₄ teaspoon minced garlic
¹/₃ cup salted roasted cashews

Remove and discard broccoli leaves and tough ends of stalks; cut into spears. Cook broccoli in a small amount of boiling water for 8 minutes or until crisp-tender. Drain well. Arrange broccoli on a serving platter. Set aside and keep warm. Melt butter in a small skillet over medium heat; add brown sugar and next 4 ingredients. Bring to a boil; remove from heat. Stir in cashews. Pour sauce over broccoli and serve immediately.

4 SERVINGS.

Vegetables & Side Dishes

Fluffy Potato Casserole

6 cups mashed potatoes	milk to mash potatoes
12 ounces cream cheese	2 eggs, beaten
2 tablespoons butter	salt
1 medium onion, chopped	1 tablespoon flour

Cook and mash potatoes. Add rest of ingredients and mix. Bake 350° for 45 minutes. Sprinkle with a can of onion rings the last 15 minutes of baking time.

Green Bean Casserole

2 cans French style green beans	1 can mushrooms, drained
1/2 pound melted grated cheese	1/2 cup bread crumbs
1/2 jar chopped pimentos	1/4 cup almonds
1 green bell pepper, chopped	6 tablespoons margarine

Melt 4 tablespoons margarine, sauté mushrooms and green peppers. Sauté almonds in 2 tablespoons margarine. Combine and mix lightly everything but almonds and bread crumbs. Pour into casserole, top with almonds and bread crumbs. Heat in oven at 350° for 20 to 30 minutes.

Vegetables & Side Dishes

Hushpuppies

1 cup self-rising white cornmeal mix	1 tablespoon sugar
½ cup self-rising flour	1 large egg, lightly beaten
½ cup diced onion	½ cup milk or beer
	vegetable oil

Combine first 4 ingredients in a large bowl. Add egg and milk in dry ingredients, stirring just until moistened. Let stand 10 minutes. Pour oil to a depth of 2 inches into a Dutch oven; heat to 375°. Drop batter by rounded tablespoonfuls into hot oil, and fry, in batches, 2 to 3 minutes on each side or until golden brown. Drain on a wire rack over paper towels; serve immediately.

Italian Vegetable Bake

1 13¼-ounce can mushrooms, drained	1 11-ounce can cut green beans, drained
1 onion, diced	1 11-ounce can yellow wax beans, drained
¼ cup butter or margarine	
1 10¾-ounce can cream of mushroom soup	1 11-ounce can sliced carrots, drained
1 10¾-ounce can cream of chicken soup	1 8-ounce package shredded Cheddar cheese
	1 8-ounce package shredded mozzarella cheese

Sauté mushrooms and onion in butter until tender, add soups, beans and carrots. Remove from heat and place into a 9x13-inch baking pan. Combine cheeses; sprinkle on top. Bake at 350° for 30 minutes or until bubbly.

12 TO 15 SERVINGS.

Vegetables & Side Dishes

Marinated Asparagus with Pecans

3	10-ounce packages frozen asparagus spears	¼	teaspoon soy sauce
¼	cup sugar	2	tablespoons cooking oil
¼	cup white vinegar	½	cup finely chopped pecans
			lettuce leaves

Cook frozen asparagus according to package directions. Place cooked asparagus in a 13x9x2-inch baking dish. Combine sugar, vinegar, soy sauce, and oil in a bowl. Stir in pecans. Pour this mixture over asparagus. Cover and chill for 8 hours. Serve drained asparagus on lettuce leaves. Drizzle with additional marinade.

8 SERVINGS.

Marinated Vegetables

1	small bottle Italian dressing		yellow bell pepper
	cherry tomatoes		purple onion
	broccoli		red bell pepper
	cauliflower	1	jar whole mushrooms
1	jar artichoke hearts		cucumbers
	jumbo green olives		baby carrots
	green bell pepper		celery
	jumbo black olives		

Clean and cut (into bite-sized pieces) a variety of the vegetables and place in a marinating bowl or a gallon sized zip-loc bag. Add a bottle of Italian salad dressing and allow to marinate overnight. Turn a few times. Enjoy!

• • • • • • • • • • • • • • • • •

Adding a variety of color makes for a more appealing and attractive dish.

• • • • • • • • • • • • • • • • •

Any vinaigrette type salad dressing will work

Vegetables & Side Dishes

Mexican Cornbread

1	pound hamburger meat or 1 pound ground sausage	1	can cream style corn
2	eggs	1	cup milk
1	cup cornmeal	1/4	cup vegetable oil
2	teaspoons baking soda	2 1/2	cups grated Cheddar cheese
1	teaspoon salt	1	medium onion, chopped
		4	jalapeño peppers, chopped

Mix all ingredients except meat and cheese in a bowl. Brown meat, set aside. Pour half of the mixture into a greased, hot skillet. Sprinkle with meat and cheese. Pour rest of mixture over the top. Bake at 350° for 45 to 50 minutes until wooden pick comes out clean.

Overnight Egg Casserole

4	cups frozen shredded hash brown potatoes, thawed	1/2	cup shredded Cheddar cheese
1	cup cubed fully cooked ham	6	eggs
1	4-ounce can chopped green chilies	1	12-ounce can evaporated milk
1/2	cup shredded Monterey Jack cheese	1/4	teaspoon pepper
			salsa, optional

In a greased 8-inch square baking dish, layer the hash browns, ham, chilies and cheeses. In a large bowl, whisk the eggs, milk and pepper; pour over the cheese. Cover and refrigerate over night. Remove from the refrigerator 30 minutes before baking. Bake, uncovered, at 350° for 1 hour or until a knife inserted near the center comes out clean. Let stand for 5 to 10 minutes. Serve with salsa if desired

9 SERVINGS.

Vegetables & Side Dishes

New South String Beans

3 cans drained green beans
1 medium onion sliced in rings
4-8 crumbled bacon pieces
1 cup light brown sugar

½ cup white vinegar
1 teaspoon dry mustard
½ teaspoon seasoned salt

Layer beans and onions in Pyrex pan. Sprinkle bacon over the top. Bring sugar, vinegar, mustard and salt to a boil. Pour over beans. Cover with aluminum foil. Bake at 350° for 45 minutes. Serve hot or cold.

Pecan Squash Casserole

4 cups yellow squash, cubed
½ cup finely chopped onion
1 10¾-ounce can cream of
mushroom soup

2 eggs
2 cups shredded Cheddar cheese
½ cup chopped pecans
1 sleeve buttery crackers, crushed

Place squash and onions in a microwave proof dish with ½-inch of water. Microwave on high for 5 minutes or until squash is tender. Drain. Preheat oven to 350°.

In a small bowl, combine soup with eggs and grated cheese. Place half the mixture in the bottom of a greased 13x9-inch baking dish. Pour half of soup mixture over squash. Sprinkle with half of the pecans. Repeat the layers. Top with crushed crackers. Bake about 30 minutes or until lightly browned.

8 SERVINGS.

Vegetables & Side Dishes

Onion Casserole

3 large purple onions (sweet
   Vidalia onions are good)
1 cup grated Cheddar cheese

2 11-ounce cans cream of onion
   soup
  potato chips, crushed

Slice onions and layer ingredients, starting with onions and ending with cheese, in a 9x12-inch casserole dish. Bake at 350° for about 45 minutes.

• • • • • • • • • • • • • •

Can substitute cream of celery soup.

Pineapple Au Gratin

2 cans pineapple chunks, drained
   leaving small amount of juice
2 cups shredded Cheddar cheese

¼ cup flour
1 cup crumbled Ritz crackers
¼ cup butter, melted

Preheat oven to 350°. Pour pineapple chunks into medium mixing bowl. Combine Cheddar cheese and flour in separate bowl until cheese is covered with flour. Mix in well with pineapple chunks. Pour into small casserole dish, sprayed with Pam. Sprinkle crumbled Ritz crackers on top and drizzle with melted butter. Bake approximately 45 minutes or until bubbling and brown around top edges.

• • • • • • • • • • • • • •

This dish can be prepared a day or two ahead and kept in refrigerator prior to baking. Wonderful as a side dish with ham, chicken or fish!!

Vegetables & Side Dishes

Potato Casserole

1 2-pound bag frozen hash brown potatoes, thawed
½ cup melted butter
1 teaspoon salt
1 teaspoon pepper

½ cup chopped onion, sauté until translucent
1 cup cream of chicken soup
1 pint sour cream
2¼ cups grated sharp Cheddar cheese

Mix first 6 ingredients well. Add sour cream and cheese. Spread in a 13x9-inch baking dish. Bake at 350° for 45 minutes.

Potato Gratin

1 onion, thinly sliced
2 tablespoons olive oil
1 tablespoon unsalted butter
2 pounds russet potatoes

2 cups plus 2 tablespoons heavy cream
2¾ cups grated Gruyère cheese
1 teaspoon salt
1 teaspoon black pepper

Preheat the oven to 350°. Spray the inside of a 10x15x2-inch baking dish with non-stick cooking spray. Sauté the onions in the olive oil and butter on medium-low heat until tender. Peel and thinly slice the potatoes. Mix the potatoes in a large bowl with 2 cups of cream, 2¼ cups of Gruyère cheese, salt, and pepper. Add the sautéed onion and mix well. Pour the potatoes into the baking dish. Press down to smooth. Combine the remaining 2 tablespoons of cream and ½ cup of Gruyère cheese and sprinkle on the top. Bake for 1½ hours, until the potatoes are tender and the top is browned and bubbly.

Vegetables & Side Dishes

Roasted Asparagus Wrapped in Prosciutto

1	pound asparagus, trimmed		freshly ground black pepper
1	tablespoon olive oil	6-8	paper thin slices prosciutto,
	salt		halved lengthwise

Preheat over to 400°. Snap dry ends off each asparagus and place on a heavy baking sheet. Drizzle with olive oil, sprinkle with salt and pepper and toss. Roast until asparagus is tender, about 15 minutes. Cool completely. Wrap each asparagus with 1 piece of prosciutto, exposing tips. Serve at room temperature.

Roasted Sweet Potatoes

3	large sweet potatoes, peeled and cut into bite-sized pieces		sea salt and black pepper, to taste
1/4	cup olive oil	2	tablespoons chopped fresh cilantro
1	teaspoon garlic, minced	2	tablespoons lime juice

Toss cut sweet potatoes with olive oil and minced garlic. Season with salt and pepper. Place sweet potatoes in a 13x9-inch pan and roast 35 minutes at 400°. Stir once or twice. Remove from oven and cool 5 minutes. Sprinkle with cilantro and lime juice. Mix to coat potatoes evenly.

Vegetables & Side Dishes

Rosemary New Potatoes

8-10 new potatoes
2 sprigs fresh rosemary
   (remove leaves from stems)
3 tablespoons olive oil
½ stick butter (2 ounces)

Parmesan cheese
salt
black pepper
Creole seasoning

Lightly boil new potatoes until they are just soft but not mushy. Cut potatoes into wedges. Drizzle a baking sheet with olive oil and sprinkle with salt, pepper, and Creole seasoning. Arrange potato wedges into a single layer and add small pieces of butter and rosemary. Sprinkle salt, pepper, Creole seasoning and Parmesan cheese, to taste, on potatoes. Bake potatoes at 425° for 15 to 18 minutes until lightly browned.

Saucy Potatoes

1 11-ounce can cream of celery
   soup
½ cup milk

1 4-ounce package cream cheese
1 8-ounce jar onions
4-6 potatoes

Preheat oven to 350°. Over low heat, combine soup and cream cheese. Slice the potatoes and put them in an 8x11-inch baking dish. Add onions. Pour the sauce over them. Cover and bake for 1 hour.

Vegetables & Side Dishes

Sausage and Chestnut Stuffing

1	pound hot sausage	2	cups chopped celery
4	cups cooked rice	1	10-ounce can chestnuts, drained
1	onion, chopped	1	can chicken broth
¼	pound mushrooms, sliced		butter

Fry sausage, drain and crumble. Sauté celery, onions, mushrooms, chestnuts in butter. Add all ingredients together and toss. Cook in baking dish at 350° for 30 minutes. Use as a side dish or as stuffing.

Sautéed Cauliflower

¼	cup olive oil		Sea salt and crushed black
½	cup diced red onion		pepper, to taste
2	cloves garlic, thinly sliced	¼	teaspoon red pepper
1	head cauliflower, cut into	¼	cup finely chopped parsley
	medium-sized florets	¼	cup plain bread crumbs

In a large pan heat oil over medium-high heat. Add onion and cook until soft. Add garlic and cook until softened, but not browned. Add cauliflower and season with salt, pepper, red pepper and parsley. Toss cauliflower in pan to coat well with oil. Sauté until cauliflower is tender. Remove from pan to individual bowls or plates and sprinkle with bread crumbs.

Sautéed Spinach with Raisins and Pine Nuts

1½	tablespoons olive oil	2	dashes fresh lemon juice
½	teaspoon minced shallots	1	teaspoon butter
½	teaspoon minced garlic	5	cups packed baby spinach
1½	tablespoons golden raisins (or currants), plumped in water		sea salt and freshly ground pepper
1½	tablespoons pine nuts, toasted		

In a medium saucepan over medium heat, add the oil and heat. Add the shallots and garlic and sauté until softened. Add the raisins and cook until warm, about 1 minute. Add the pine nuts, increase the heat, and add the lemon juice. Stir with a wooden spoon to scrape up the browned bits that cling to the bottom of the pan. Add the butter and melt, then add the spinach and stir or toss with tongs until wilted. Season with salt and pepper, to taste.

Shoe Peg Corn Casserole

1	can shoe peg corn	1	11-ounce can cream of chicken soup
1	can French style green beans, drained	1	4-ounce container sour cream
½	onion, diced	1	8-ounce package shredded Cheddar cheese
½	bell pepper, diced	1	tube buttered crackers, crushed fine
1	11-ounce can cream of celery soup	1	stick butter, melted

Combine all ingredients, except butter and crackers in casserole dish. Pour melted butter over top of mixture followed by crackers and bake uncovered for 1 hour at 350°.

Vegetables & Side Dishes

Sliced Baked Potatoes

4 medium potatoes	4 tablespoons grated Cheddar cheese
2-3 tablespoons chopped chives, parsley, thyme or sage	2-3 tablespoons butter
1 teaspoon salt	1½ tablespoons grated Parmesan cheese

Peel potatoes if skin is tough, otherwise rinse and dry. Cut potatoes into thin slices, but not all the way through. Place potatoes in microwave dish and sprinkle with melted butter and herbs. Microwave at high power for 10 minutes, turning after 5 minutes. Let rest for 5 minutes and sprinkle with grated cheese and Parmesan. Microwave another 4 to 6 minutes on high until soft and cheese melts.

Spinach Crumb Casserole

1 10-ounce package frozen chopped spinach, thawed and squeezed dry	1 tablespoon chopped onion
	½ teaspoon salt
2 eggs, beaten	1 cup soft bread crumbs
½ cup milk	4½ teaspoons butter or margarine, melted
½ cup cubed process cheese	

In a large bowl, combine the spinach, eggs, milk, cheese, onion and salt. Pour into a greased 1-quart baking dish. Combine bread crumbs and butter, sprinkle over the top. Bake, uncovered, at 350° for 25 to 30 minutes or until a knife inserted near the center comes out clean.

4 SERVINGS.

Vegetables & Side Dishes

Southern Sweet Potato Casserole

2	cans sweet potatoes drained
1/2	cup milk
11	tablespoons butter divided
1	cup sugar
2	eggs
1	tablespoon vanilla

1	teaspoon ground cinnamon
1/2	teaspoon salt
1	cup packed brown sugar
1	cup chopped pecans
1/3	cup all-purpose flour

Preheat the oven to 350°. Place sweet potatoes in large bowl. Add milk and 3 tablespoons butter. Beat with electric mixer on low until fluffy. Add sugar, eggs, vanilla, cinnamon, and salt; beat until mixed. Spread in a greased 3-quart casserole. For topping stir together brown sugar, pecans, and flour. Melt remaining 8 tablespoons butter; stir into pecan mixture until mixed. Sprinkle topping evenly over sweet potatoes. Bake for 30 minutes.

12 SERVINGS.

Sweet Potato Casserole

4	cups fresh mashed sweet potatoes
1	cup sugar
1	stick melted butter

1	teaspoon vanilla
1/3	cup milk
4	large eggs, beaten

Topping

1/2	cup firmly packed brown sugar
1/4	cup flour

2 1/2	tablespoons butter
1	cup chopped pecans

Beat casserole ingredients in mixer until well blended. Put into a well-greased 2-quart long casserole dish. Mix and spread topping ingredients over the sweet potato mixture. Bake at 350° for 60 minutes (325° for a glass dish).

Vegetables & Side Dishes

Spinach Casserole

2 10-ounce packages spinach
½ jar pasteurized process cheese
    sauce

½ teaspoon butter
1 cup sour cream
    salt and pepper, to taste

Cook spinach, drain well and add cheese sauce. Stir to melt then add sour cream and butter. Pour into casserole dish. Bake at 350° for 25 minutes.

Stuffed Baked Potatoes

4 baked (or microwaved) potatoes
    salt and pepper
½ stick butter
    garlic powder
½ cup sour cream

    parsley
¼ cup mayonnaise
    milk — just a dash
1 egg

Topping
    cheese
    bacon bits

    chives

Slice each of the 4 potatoes in half long ways. Scoop out the potato with maybe a ¼ left around the skin. Place skins on a cookie sheet and set aside. In a large bowl mix potatoes, butter, sour cream, mayonnaise and the egg. Add salt, pepper, garlic powder and parsley, to taste. A small amount of milk will need to be added to make the texture creamier. Fill potato skins with this mixture and bake in 350° oven for 20 minutes. Add toppings of cheese, bacon and chives during the last 5 minutes, just long enough to melt the cheese.

Vegetables & Side Dishes

Tomato Pie

1   package crescent dinner rolls
3-4 tomatoes, sliced (soak up juice
      with paper towel)
      green onions, chopped
2   tablespoons basil

      salt and pepper
1   cup mayonnaise
1   cup grated Monterey Jack
      cheese

Blend basil, salt and pepper together, set to side. Mix cheese and mayonnaise together, set to side. Layer pie pan with crescent rolls to make crust, layer tomatoes, basil, salt and pepper, layer mayonnaise-cheese mixture. Bake 20 minutes in a 425° oven.

Thyme Green Beans with Almonds

2   pounds fresh green beans
1/2 teaspoon salt
2   tablespoon butter or margarine
1/2 teaspoon pepper

1   tablespoon minced fresh or dried
      thyme
1/3 cup slivered almonds, toasted

Place beans in a steamer basket. Place in saucepan over 1-inch of water; bring to boil. Cover and steam for 10 to 12 minutes or until crisp-tender. In a large skillet, melt butter; add the beans, thyme, salt and pepper. Cook and stir for 5 minutes or until heated through. Sprinkle with almonds.

8 SERVINGS.

Vegetables & Side Dishes

Vegetable Casserole

1	15-ounce can white corn	2	cups grated Cheddar cheese
1	14.5-ounce can French style green beans	³/₄	cup melted butter
1	10.75-ounce can chicken mushroom soup	1¹/₂	stacks buttery crackers (crushed)
1	8-ounce package sour cream		chopped white onions and bell pepper, to taste
1	3-ounce can water chestnuts		

Mix corn, green beans, soup, sour cream, water chestnuts, onions, bell pepper and cheese in a bowl. Place mixture in greased 9x12x2-inch baking dish. Mix crackers and melted butter and sprinkle on top of vegetables. Bake in 350° over for 35 minutes.

French Toast Casserole

5	cups bread cubes	¹/₄	teaspoon salt
4	eggs	1	teaspoon vanilla extract
1¹/₂	cups milk	1	tablespoon margarine, softened
³/₄	cup white sugar, divided	1	teaspoon ground cinnamon

Preheat oven to 350°. Lightly butter an 8x8-inch baking pan. Line bottom of pan with bread cubes. In a large bowl, beat together eggs, milk, 2 tablespoons sugar, salt and vanilla, pour egg mixture over bread. Dot with margarine; let stand for 10 minutes. Combine remaining 2 tablespoons sugar with 1 teaspoon cinnamon and sprinkle over the top. Bake in preheated oven about 45 to 50 minutes, until top is golden.

Vegetables & Side Dishes

Mimi's Cornbread

1½ cups cornmeal
2 cups buttermilk
1 stick margarine or butter
1 teaspoon salt

1 teaspoon baking soda
1 egg
3 tablespoons flour

Melt butter in iron skillet. Mix all ingredients well. Pour melted butter into mixture, combine. Pour into iron skillet and bake at 350° until wooden pick comes out clean and browned on top.

Walnut Cream Pasta

1 12-ounce package fettuccine
¼ cup heavy whipping cream
2 garlic cloves, minced
¼ teaspoon salt
3 tablespoons butter

⅛ teaspoon pepper
½ cup chicken broth
1 cup grated Parmesan cheese
¼ cup sour cream
1 cup finely chopped walnuts

Cook the fettuccine according to package directions. Meanwhile in a small saucepan, sauté garlic in butter for 1 minute. Gradually stir in broth. Reduce heat. In a bowl, combine sour cream, whipping cream, salt and pepper; stir into broth mixture (do not boil). Drain fettuccine and place in large serving bowl. Add the cream sauce, Parmesan cheese and walnuts; toss to coat.

6 SERVINGS.

Vegetables & Side Dishes

Sour Cream Biscuits

1	stick melted butter	1	8-ounce carton sour cream
1	tablespoon buttermilk	2	cups biscuit mix

Preheat oven to 425°. Grease miniature muffin tins. Combine ingredients and blend thoroughly with a fork. Drop into miniature muffin tins and bake 12 minutes.

3 DOZEN MUFFINS.

Zucchini Dressing

4	medium zucchini, sliced ½-inch thick	½	cup chopped onion
4	tablespoons butter	½	cup sour cream
¾	cup shredded carrots	1	can cream of chicken soup
		1	box chicken flavor stuffing mix

Preheat oven to 350°. Cook zucchini in butter until tender. Remove. Cook onions and carrots in butter until onions are clear. Prepare stuffing mix according to package directions. Add sour cream and soup to the stuffing. Stir to mix. Add the onions and carrots to the mixture. Stir. Gently stir in zucchini. Spoon into casserole dish. Bake for 30 to 40 minutes.

Zucchini with Pecans

	vegetable cooking spray	½	teaspoon olive oil
⅛	tablespoon garlic salt	2	tablespoons chopped pecans, toasted
1½	cups julienne strips zucchini		
⅛	teaspoon white pepper		

Coat skillet with cooking spray; sauté zucchini in oil until crisp-tender. Add remaining ingredients, tossing gently.

2 SERVINGS.

Vegetables & Side Dishes

Notes

Notes

Desserts

Cakes, Cobblers,
Puddings, Cookies,
Cheesecakes,
Tarts, Brownies, etc.

Apple Cake

1 cup self-rising flour, put aside	1 teaspoon vanilla extract
½ cup	2 cups chopped pecans
2 cups sugar	1½ cups vegetable oil
3 teaspoons cinnamon	3 large apples, chopped
2 eggs	

Coat apples in ½ cup flour. Mix dry ingredients first then add oil and eggs, mix well. Add flour coated apples and nuts. Bake in a greased and floured tube pan at 325° for approximately 1 hour or until wooden pick comes out clean.

Apple-Gingerbread Cobbler

1 14-ounce package gingerbread mix, divided	½ cup butter, divided
¾ cup water	½ cup chopped pecans
¼ cup firmly packed light brown sugar	2 21-ounce cans apple pie filling vanilla ice cream

Stir together 2 cups gingerbread mix and ¾ cup water until smooth; set mixture aside. Stir together remaining gingerbread mix and brown sugar; cut in ¼ cup butter until mixture is crumbly. Stir in chopped pecans; set pecan mixture aside. Combine apple pie filling and remaining ¼ cup butter in a large sauce and cook, stirring often, 5 minutes over medium heat or until thoroughly heated. Spoon hot apple pie filling mixture, evenly, into a lightly greased 11x7-inch baking dish. Spoon gingerbread mixture evenly over hot apple pie filling mixture; sprinkle evenly with pecan and brown sugar mixture. Bake at 375° for 30 to 35 minutes, or until set. Serve cobbler with vanilla ice cream.

8 SERVINGS.

Desserts

Apple Streusel Cobbler

2	cans apple pie filling	½	cup firmly packed brown sugar
2	eggs	½	cup flour
1	can sweetened condensed milk	¼	cup cold margarine
¼	cup margarine, melted	½	cup chopped nuts
½	teaspoon cinnamon	½	cup oats
¼	teaspoon nutmeg		

Preheat oven to 375°. Spread apple pie filling in buttered 9-inch square baking pan. Beat eggs. Add sweetened condensed milk, melted margarine, cinnamon and nutmeg; mix well. Pour over apple filling. In medium bowl combine sugar and flour, cut in margarine until crumbly. Add nuts and oats, sprinkle over custard. Bake 50 to 55 minutes until set. Let cool. Serve with ice cream.

Apricot Nectar Cake

1	box lemon supreme cake mix	4	eggs
½	cup vegetable oil	1	cup canned apricot nectar
½	cup sugar		

Mix the above well and bake at 300° for approximately 1 hour or until done.

Icing

½	cup lemon juice	1½ cups confectioners' sugar

Mix the following well and pour over top of cake.

Bananas Foster Bread Pudding

Bread Pudding

½	cup whole pecans	2	large ripe bananas, peeled, mashed with a fork
1	loaf French bread, cut into 1-inch cubes	¼	cup dried apricots chopped into ¼-inch pieces, optional
3	large eggs, lightly beaten	1	tablespoon vanilla extract
2	cups milk	1	tablespoon ground cinnamon
⅔	cup sugar	¼	teaspoon nutmeg, ground (preferably freshly grated)

Preheat oven to 350°. Place pecans on cookie sheet and lightly toast in oven 4 to 6 minutes. Set aside to cool, and roughly chop. Lightly butter a deep 9x12-inch baking dish and add the bread cubes in an even layer. In a large bowl, whisk together the eggs, milk, sugar, mashed bananas, vanilla, cinnamon, and nutmeg. Pour the mixture over the bread cubes. Gently fold in the pecans and dried apricot pieces. Cover the dish with aluminum foil. Place the dish in the refrigerator for 30 minutes to an hour to allow the liquid soak into the bread. Preheat oven to 325° and place bread pudding on a middle rack. Leave the aluminum foil on. Bake for 45 minutes. Remove the foil and bake for another 20 to 30 minutes until firm and a knife inserted comes out clean.

Rum Sauce

½	cup dark rum	1	teaspoon ground cinnamon
¼	cup banana liqueur, optional	5	large bananas, peeled and quartered
½	stick butter, unsalted		
1	cup dark brown sugar		

While the bread pudding is baking, heat up the butter in a large skillet over medium heat. When the butter begins to melt add the brown sugar, cinnamon, and quartered bananas. Sauté gently, moving the bananas around, for about 1 minute. Remove the skillet from heat and add the rum and liqueur. Return the skillet to medium heat. When the liquid begins to bubble, tilt the pan and using caution, light the sauce with a long match. When the flames go away,

Desserts

Bananas Foster Bread Pudding – continued

remove the skillet from heat. (If you can't get the sauce to light, just cook for 3 to 4 minutes to allow the alcohol to burn off.) The rum sauce should be served warm. If it cools down to much, reheat in a saucepan over low heat or in a microwave.

Whipped Cream

1   cup heavy whipping cream, cold   ½   teaspoon vanilla extract
2   tablespoons sugar

Whip the cream until it just begins to thicken. Add the vanilla and sprinkle the sugar over the cream. Continue to whip until soft peaks form. Use immediately or refrigerate.

• • • • • • • • • • • • • • • • •

Scoop out the bread pudding and place serving on plate or bowl. Add 2 pieces of cooked bananas and drizzle the rum sauce over the top. Add whipped cream.

Banana Bread

2   sticks butter or margarine   3-4   very ripe bananas
1   cup sugar   1½   cups flour
2   eggs, beaten   1   teaspoon baking soda
¾   cup chopped nuts, optional

Cream butter and sugar. Add beaten eggs. Cream bananas until fluffy. Mix flour and baking soda. Gradually add bananas to butter mixture alternating with dry ingredients. Add nuts at this time if desired. Pour into greased loaf pan. Bake at 350° for 45 minutes to 1 hour. Bread is ready when toothpick inserted in middle comes out clean. Allow to cool slightly, and then turn out on foil until completely cooled.

Desserts

Banana Nut Bundt Cake/Bread

1	cup shortening	3	cups all-purpose flour
3	cups sugar	1½	teaspoons baking soda
4	eggs	¼	teaspoon salt
¼	cup buttermilk	6	small bananas, mashed
2	tablespoons vanilla extract	1½	cups chopped pecans

Cream shortening and sugar until light and fluffy. Add eggs, one at a time, beating well after each addition. Add buttermilk and vanilla extract; blend thoroughly until smooth. Then combine flour, baking soda, and salt; add to creamed mixture. Add mashed bananas and pecans. Mix just until blended. Spoon batter into a lightly greased, 10-inch Bundt pan. Bake at 325° for 1 hour and 20 minutes or until cake tests done. This cake is very moist!

Better Than Sex Cake

1	box yellow cake mix	½	cup water
1	small box instant vanilla pudding, dry	1	German sweetened chocolate bar, shredded
4	eggs	1	6-ounce package chocolate bits
1	8-ounce carton sour cream	1	cup chopped pecans
½	cup oil		

Mix first 6 ingredients together and beat with electric mixer until smooth; add next 3 ingredients. Pour batter into greased and floured Bundt pan. Bake at 325° for 55 minutes. Use toothpick for doneness. Let cool; remove from pan. Keep covered with foil or wrap for freshness.

Desserts

Banana Split Dessert

2 cups graham cracker crumbs	1 8-ounce tub whipped topping, thawed
1/2 cup melted butter or margarine	
1 8-ouunce package cream cheese	8 medium strawberries, halved
1 cup confectioners' sugar	1/4 cup chopped pecans
4 large bananas	1 tablespoon chocolate syrup
1 20-ounce can crushed pineapple, drained	

Combine graham cracker crumbs and melted butter. Press evenly and firmly into the bottom of a 13x9-inch dish. In a medium bowl, combine cream cheese and sugar. Blend until smooth. Spoon evenly over crumb crust. Slice bananas and arrange on top of cream cheese layer. Spoon pineapple over bananas. Spread whipped topping over pineapple. Arrange strawberry halves on top and sprinkle with nuts. Drizzle with chocolate syrup. Cover and refrigerate 4 to 8 hours.

Bing Cherry Parfait

1/2 gallon vanilla ice cream, softened	1 cup chopped pecans
2 dozen crumbled macaroons	1/2 cup bourbon
1 can Bing cherries, drained and halved	whipped cream

Soak cherries in bourbon for 24 hours. Add all ingredients to ice cream, folding macaroons and pecans. Freeze in parfaits. Top with whipped cream. Do not take out until ready to serve.

Blueberry Crunch

1	20-ounce can crushed pineapple in juice, undrained	½	cup sugar
1	18.25-ounce box yellow cake mix	½	cup butter, melted
3	cups fresh blueberries	1	cup chopped pecans

Preheat oven to 350°. Spread pineapple in a lightly buttered 13x9-inch dish. Sprinkle with dry cake mix. Add blueberries, and then sprinkle with sugar. Top with pecans and drizzle with melted butter. Bake approximately 50 minutes, or until bubbly.

• • • • • • • • • • • • • • • •

Frozen blueberries may be used, however, thaw completely before using and drain all excess water.

Brownie Pizza

1	20-ounce box chocolate brownie mix	3	tablespoons sugar
1	8-ounce package cream cheese, softened	2	bananas, sliced and tossed in lemon juice to prevent browning
1	8-ounce can crushed pineapple, drained	1	cup strawberries, sliced
		1	cup chopped pecans
			chocolate syrup for drizzling

Preheat oven to 350°. Grease a 15-inch pizza pan. Prepare brownie mix according to directions on box. Pour onto prepared pan. Bake for 20 minutes or until done. Remove from oven and cool. Beat cream cheese, pineapple and sugar together to a good spreading consistency. Spread mixture over cooled brownie crust. Arrange banana and strawberry slices over cream cheese mixture. Sprinkle with chopped pecans and drizzle with chocolate syrup. Refrigerate. Slice as you would a pizza to serve.

Desserts

Bourbon Balls

1	cup pecans	3	tablespoons cocoa
3	cups crushed vanilla wafers	2	tablespoons light corn syrup
1	cup confectioners' sugar	½	cup bourbon

Grind pecans and vanilla wafers in blender. Mix with sugar and cocoa. Stir light corn syrup into bourbon and pour onto dry ingredients. Mix all until moistened then shape into very small balls. Roll in confectioners' sugar.

Brownies

1⅓	cups flour	2	cups sugar
½	teaspoon salt	4	eggs
1	teaspoon baking powder	1½	teaspoons vanilla extract
1	cup butter	2	cups chopped nuts
1½	cups unsweetened cocoa powder		

Preheat oven to 350°. Grease a 9x13-inch pan. With a wire whisk stir flour, salt and baking powder together. Mix well. Set aside. Melt butter. Stir in cocoa powder. Stir well. Add sugar. Beat in eggs one a time. Stir in vanilla extract. Add premixed flour mixture. Mix well. Stir in chopped nuts. Bake in prepared pan for 30 minutes. Remove from oven and cool on wire rack. Ice with chocolate frosting when completely cool.

Fudge Icing

¼	cup butter, melted	2	cups confectioners' sugar, sifted
⅔	cup cocoa powder	¼	cup milk
½	teaspoon vanilla extract		

In double boiler mix butter and cocoa powder. Stir in vanilla extract. Add confectioners' sugar and enough milk to make a thick, but spreadable icing. Spread on cooled brownies before icing hardens.

Desserts

Buffalo Chip Cookies

1 cup butter, softened	1 cup chopped nuts
1 cup brown sugar	1 cup chopped dates
1 cup granulated sugar	1 small bag chocolate chips
2 eggs	2 cups plain flour
1½ teaspoons baking powder	1 teaspoon baking soda
2 cups Wheaties cereal	2 cups oatmeal

Mix butter, brown sugar, granulated sugar, egg, flour and baking powder. Mix well. Add other ingredients and mix well. Drop on a lightly greased cookie sheet. Bake at 350° for 10 to 12 minutes. Cool on rack.

3 DOZEN.

Butter Fingers

1 cup butter, softened	1 6-ounce package semi-sweet chocolate morsels
½ cup sifted confectioners' sugar	
1 teaspoon vanilla extract	1 tablespoon shortening
2 cups all-purpose flour	½ cup finely chopped nuts, optional

Cream butter and gradually add sugar, beating until fluffy. Stir in vanilla extract and gradually add flour, mix well. Shape dough into 2½x2½-inch "fingers" and place on an ungreased cookie sheet. Flatten ¾ of each cookie with the tines of a fork. Bake at 350° for 12 to 15 minutes until lightly browned. Remove to racks and cool. Melt morsels and shortening in the top of a double boiler. Leave chocolate over hot water while working on each cookie. Dip the unflattened tip of each cookie into the chocolate and, if desired, roll in the nuts.

• • • • • • • • • • • • • • • •

Will keep well in an airtight container, separating each layer of cookies with waxed paper.

Desserts

Buttermilk Pie

1	9-inch pie shell, unbaked	3	eggs, beaten
½	cup butter, softened	1	cup buttermilk
2	cups sugar	1	teaspoon vanilla extract
3	tablespoons flour		

Cream butter and sugar with mixer. Add flour and eggs and beat well. Stir in buttermilk and vanilla extract. Pour filling into pie shell. Bake on lower rack of oven at 350° for 45 to 50 minutes. Place on wire rack and let cool completely before serving.

Caramel Coffee Cake

1	package frozen roll dough	1	cup chopped pecans
1	stick margarine, melted	1	cup brown sugar
2	4-ounce packages butterscotch cook pudding (NOT INSTANT!)	1	teaspoon cinnamon

Place frozen rolls evenly inside greased Bundt or tube pan. They will be piled up on top of each other. Drizzle 1 stick of melted margarine over rolls. Pour dry pudding mix over top of margarine. Next sprinkle a cup of firmly packed brown sugar and a teaspoon or so of cinnamon over this. Then sprinkle the pecans over the top of all. Place pan on a cookie or jelly-roll pan. Place a piece of wax paper or plastic wrap and a dish towel over the pan. Place in an unheated oven overnight. The next morning, remove the pan and take the towel and paper off the top. Preheat the oven to 350°. Bake for 30 minutes. You may want to put foil over the top for the last 5 minutes. Remove from oven and invert on plate. Let stand 2 to 3 minutes.

• • • • • • • • • • • • • • • • •

Do not put overnight in a gas oven. Set in a draft free area on counter.

Desserts

Candy Bar Cheesecake

Crust

1½ cups chocolate graham cracker crumbs

6 tablespoons butter, melted

2 tablespoons sugar

Preheat oven to 350°. Wrap aluminum foil under and around outside of a 9-inch springform pan. For crust, combine cracker crumbs, melted butter and sugar in a medium bowl; stir until well blended. Press into bottom and halfway up the sides of prepared pan. Bake 50 minutes; cool completely.

Filling

4 8-ounce packages cream cheese, softened

1 cup firmly packed brown sugar

3 eggs

1 tablespoon vanilla extract

2 chocolate covered caramel, peanut, and nougat candy bars, chopped

2 tablespoons caramel ice cream topping

Preheat oven to 350°. For filling, beat cream cheese in a large bowl until fluffy. Gradually beat in brown sugar. Add eggs, 1 at a time, beating well after each addition. Stir in vanilla extract. Pour batter over crust (see above). Bake 1 hour or until filling is set. Sprinkle with chopped candy bars. Bake 7 minutes or until candy softens. Cool on wire rack. Remove sides of pan. Drizzle with caramel topping. Store in airtight container in refrigerator.

10 TO 12 SERVINGS.

Caramel Pound Cake

Cake

3½ cups all-purpose flour	1¼ cups granulated sugar
1 teaspoon baking powder	1½ cups butter, softened
½ teaspoon salt	6 large eggs
2 cups firmly packed light brown sugar	1¼ cups milk

Preheat oven to 325°. Grease and flour a 10-inch tube or Bundt pan. Sift the flour, baking powder, and salt together. In a large mixing bowl, cream the 2 sugars and butter with a mixer, and then add eggs, one at a time, beating well after each addition. Alternately, add flour and milk to the creamed mixture and beat until well blended and smooth. Scrape into the prepared pan and bake until a knife inserted into the cake comes out almost clean, about 1 hour (be careful not to over bake). Transfer to a wire rack, cool 10 minutes, then turn out onto rack and cool completely.

Icing

½ cup butter	½ cup milk
1 cup firmly packed dark brown sugar	½ teaspoon vanilla extract
	4 cups confectioners' sugar

Melt the butter in a large, heavy saucepan over low heat. Add brown sugar and milk and stir until it almost reaches a boil. Remove from heat and let cool. Stir in vanilla extract and gradually add the confectioners' sugar. Stir until well blended and very smooth. Transfer cake to cake plate and frost the top and sides using a heavy knife. Let cake stand at least 1 hour before serving.

Keeps very well for several days in the refrigerator.

Desserts

Carrot Cake

1½	cups vegetable oil	2	teaspoons baking soda
2	cups sugar	2	teaspoons baking powder
4	eggs, beaten	3	cups grated carrots
2	cups all-purpose flour	1	cup chopped pecans
2	teaspoons cinnamon		

Preheat oven to 350°. Blend oil and sugar well. Add eggs. Sift flour, cinnamon, baking soda, and baking powder. Blend into mixture a little at a time. Fold in carrots and nuts. Bake approximately 30 minutes in 3 buttered, floured round cake pans.

Frosting

1	8-ounce package cream cheese	2	tablespoons vanilla extract
1	stick butter	1	box confectioners' sugar

Mix together cream cheese, butter and vanilla extract. Add sugar a little at a time. Wait until cake cools completely before adding the frosting.

Chocolate Brownie Trifle

1	box brownie mix	4	cups milk
3	small boxes instant chocolate pudding	3	chocolate covered toffee bars
		1	large tub whipped topping

Bake brownies as directed on package and crumble. Prepare chocolate pudding as directed on package. Layer ⅓ of brownies, pudding, whipped topping and toffee pieces. Repeat layers 2 more times. Refrigerate at least 3 hours.

Desserts

Chess Squares

1	box yellow cake mix	1	stick margarine, melted
1	egg		

Mix and pat into 9x13-inch pan. Bake in a 350° oven for 30 to 45 minutes.

Frosting

1	box confectioners' sugar	2	eggs
1	8-ounce package cream cheese, softened		

Blend frosting ingredients together until smooth. Spread on cake mixture.

Chocolate Chip Cake

1	box yellow butter cake mix	1	cup oil
1	small box chocolate instant pudding	4	eggs
1	8-ounce container sour cream	1	6-ounce package semi-sweet chocolate chips
¼	cup water	1	cup chopped pecans, optional

Preheat over to 350°. Grease and flour large sheet cake pan or a 3-quart glass dish. Bake for 35 to 40 minutes. Spread icing over cake and cut in to squares.

Chocolate Icing

1	stick butter
2	tablespoons cocoa
5-6	tablespoons milk

1	box confectioners' sugar
1	teaspoon vanilla extract

Melt butter in a saucepan. Add cocoa, milk and confectioners' sugar. Cook until smooth. Remove from heat and stir in vanilla extract. Pour over cake.

20 TO 25 SERVINGS.

Desserts

Cheese Cake Squares

Crust

3   tablespoons butter   ¼   cup sugar
1   cup graham cracker crumbs

Mix together graham cracker crumbs butter and sugar. Line a 9x13-inch pan with mixture, slightly building up sides, and bake at 375° for 8 minutes.

Filling

3   8-ounce packages cream cheese,   ¾   cup sugar
    softened   1½ tablespoons vanilla extract
5   eggs

Cream together cream cheese and sugar. Add eggs and vanilla extract. Beat until smooth. Pour over prepared crust. Bake at 325° for 40 minutes. Remove from oven and set aside. Increase oven temperature to 425°.

Topping

1   pint sour cream   ½   teaspoon vanilla extract
¼   cup sugar

Mix together topping ingredients. Pour over cheesecake. Return to oven for 8 to 10 minutes. Chill well and cut into squares.

Chocolate Covered Espresso Beans

1   cup espresso beans
1   12-ounce package dark chocolate
    chips

1   12-ounce package semi-sweet
    chocolate chips

Melt chips according to package directions and mix thoroughly. Place espresso beans about ½-inch apart on a waxed cookie sheet. Spoon chocolate over the beans. Chill in refrigerator until hardened. Turn beans over and spoon chocolate one more time over beans. Chill until hardened.

Chocolate Nut Clusters

1   24-ounce package chocolate
    almond bark

1   12-ounce package semi-sweet
    chocolate chips
1   24-ounce can salted peanuts

In a large microwave safe bowl, heat almond bark and chips on defrost until melted, 2 minutes at a time for about 6 minutes. Stir in peanuts and spoon onto waxed paper in small mounds.

30 TO 36 PIECES.

Congo Squares

1   box light brown sugar
1   package semi-sweet chocolate
    chips
¾   cup melted shortening

2¾ cups self-rising flour
4   eggs
1   cup chopped nuts
2   tablespoons vanilla extract

Mix eggs, brown sugar and melted shortening. Gradually add flour and stir. Add chocolate chips and chopped nuts. Mix thoroughly. Spread mixture on a greased cookie sheet and bake at 325° for 25 minutes. Let cool and serve.

Desserts

Chocolate Pecan Torte

1	cup butter, melted	½	cup all-purpose flour
1½	cups sugar	3	tablespoons water
1½	teaspoons vanilla extract	¾	cup finely chopped pecans
3	eggs, separated	⅛	teaspoon cream of tartar
⅔	cup Hershey's cocoa	⅛	teaspoon salt

Royal Glaze

1⅓ cups semi-sweet chocolate chips   ½ cup whipped topping

Line bottom of 9-inch springform pan with aluminum foil. Butter foil and side of pan. Heat oven to 350°. In large mixing bowl, combine butter, sugar, and vanilla extract. Beat well. Add egg yolks, one at a time, beating well after each addition. Blend in cocoa, flour and water; beat well. Stir in chopped pecans. In small mixing bowl, beat egg whites, cream of tartar and salt until stiff peaks form. Carefully fold into chocolate mixture. Pour into prepared pan. Bake 45 minutes or until top begins to crack slightly. (Cake will not test done in center.) Cool 1 hour. Cover and chill until firm. Remove side of pan. Pour Royal Glaze over cake, allowing glaze to run down side. Spread glaze evenly on top and side. Allow to set. Garnish with pecan halves, optional.

Royal Glaze: in small saucepan combine 1⅓ cups semi-sweet chocolate chips and ½ cup whipping cream. Cook over low heat stirring constantly, until chips are melted and mixture begins to thicken.

Desserts

Chocolate Truffles

³/4 cup semi-sweet chocolate chips
¹/4 cup light corn syrup
2 tablespoons amaretto or bourbon
2 cups finely crushed chocolate cookies (scrap out the middle filling)

1 cup confectioners' sugar
1 cup chopped pecans or walnuts
chocolate sprinkles
¹/4 cup brewed coffee

Heat chocolate chips, coffee, corn syrup, and liquor over low heat until melted and smooth. Stir in cookie crumbs, confectioners' sugar, and nuts. Mix well and let stand 10 minutes or until cool enough to shape. Shape into balls (the size of a boulder marble). Roll in sprinkles and let stand until fully cool.

Cookie Bars

¹/2 cup butter
1¹/2 cups graham cracker crumbs
1 14-ounce can sweetened condensed milk

1 6-ounce package semi-sweet chocolate chips
1¹/3 cups flaked coconut
1 cup chopped nuts

Preheat oven to 350° (325° for glass dish). In 13x9-inch pan, melt margarine in oven. Sprinkle cracker crumbs over margarine. Pour condensed milk evenly over crumbs. Top with remaining ingredients and press down. Bake about 25 minutes or until lightly browned. Cool and cut into bars. Store at room temperature.

Desserts

Cream Cheese Pound Cake

2	sticks butter	6	large eggs
1	stick margarine	3	cups cake flour
1	8-ounce package cream cheese	1	tablespoon vanilla extract
3	cups sugar		

Preheat oven to 325°. Cream butter, margarine, cream cheese, and sugar until smooth. Add eggs alternately with flour, beating well after each addition. Stir in vanilla extract. Pour batter into a well-greased tube pan. Bake for 90 minutes, and cool in pan for 10 minutes before turning out.

Cream Cheese Tarts

1	8-ounce package cream cheese, softened	2	eggs
1	cup sugar	12	vanilla wafers
1¼	teaspoons vanilla extract	1	21-ounce can any pie filling

Preheat oven to 350°. Place a paper cupcake liner in each cup of a muffin tin. Beat cream cheese until fluffy. Add sugar and vanilla and beat well. Add eggs, one at a time, beating well after each addition. Lay a vanilla wafer, flat side down, in each muffin cup. Spoon cream cheese mixture over wafers. Bake for 20 minutes. Allow tarts to cool completely. Serve with pie filling on top.

Desserts

Crème De Menthe Brownies

¼	cup butter, softened	4	eggs
½	teaspoon salt	1	cup all-purpose flour
1	cup sugar	1	teaspoon vanilla extract
1	16-ounce can chocolate syrup		

Cream butter with sugar until light and fluffy. Add eggs, beating well. Combine flour and salt. Add to above, alternating with syrup. Begin and end with flour. Stir in vanilla. Bake at 350° for 25 to 30 minutes in a 9x13-inch greased and floured pan. Cool well.

1st Topping

¼	cup butter	2	cups confectioners' sugar
2	tablespoons crème de menthe (GREEN) important		

Cream butter, sugar, and crème de menthe. Mix well and spread over brownies. Chill well.

2nd Topping

¼	cup butter	1	6-ounce package semi-sweet chocolate morsels

Combine chocolate and butter in double boiler. Melt and spread over brownies. Then chill before cutting into 1-inch squares.

Crème Puffs

Puffs

½ cup water
⅓ cup margarine
⅔ cup flour

dash of salt
2 eggs

Bring water and margarine to a boil. Add flour and salt, stirring vigorously over low heat until mixture forms a ball. Remove from heat. Add eggs, one at a time, beating until smooth after each addition. Place level measuring tablespoonfuls of batter on ungreased cookie sheet. Bake at 400° for 25 minutes. Cool. When ready to fill, cut tops and core the dough out of the puff. Fill with custard. Top with melted chocolate and slivered almonds. Unfilled puffs can be prepared weeks before and frozen if wrapped securely and without moisture.

Custard Filling

2 eggs
1 teaspoon vanilla extract
¼ teaspoon almond extract
1 cup confectioners' sugar

1 quart half-and-half
4 teaspoons flour
4 tablespoons cornstarch

In large saucepan, mix egg yolks, confectioners' sugar, almond extract and vanilla. Add half-and-half, always stirring. Slowly add cornstarch 1 tablespoon at a time. Then add flour. Cook on medium heat, stirring constantly until thick. Cool for 2 hours in refrigerator.

Topping

½ package melted chocolate

½ cup almond slivers

Place on top of cream puffs.

Decadent Mud Pie

1   11³/4-ounce jar hot fudge sauce,
      heated and divided
1   9-ounce graham cracker crust
¹/2 gallon coffee ice cream, softened

frozen whipped topping, thawed
blanched slivered almonds,
  toasted

Spread ¹/3 cup fudge sauce over crust. Spread ice cream over fudge sauce; cover and freeze until firm. Let pie stand at room temperature for 5 minutes before slicing. Cut into wedges. Top each serving with remaining fudge sauce, whipped topping and almonds. Serve immediately.

Derby Pie

1   9-inch pastry crust
3   eggs, lightly beaten
³/4 cup light corn syrup
3   tablespoons sugar
3   tablespoons brown sugar
3   tablespoons butter, softened

1   teaspoon vanilla
¹/4 teaspoon salt
¹/2 cup finely chopped pecans
¹/3 cup bourbon
1   cup chocolate chips
1¹/2 cups pecan halves

Preheat oven to 350° degrees. Mix all ingredients except chocolate chips. Stir in chopped pecans and bourbon. Pat chocolate chips into the bottom of pastry, then pour filling over them. Arrange pecan halves on top. Bake about 1 hour or until knife inserted in the center comes out clean. Serve with whipped cream.

Divinity

2½ cups sugar
½   cup light corn syrup

2   eggs
1   teaspoon vanilla extract

In a 2-quart saucepan combine sugar, corn syrup, ¼ teaspoon salt and ½ cup water. Cook to hard ball stage (260°); stirring only till sugar dissolves. In the meantime, beat egg whites to stiff peaks. Gradually pour syrup over egg whites, beating at high speed on electric mixer. Add vanilla and beat till candy holds its shape, about 5 minutes. Quickly drop from a teaspoon onto waxed paper.

40 PIECES.

Easy Bake Cookies

1   18¼-ounce package yellow cake
    mix
½   cup vegetable oil
2   large eggs

1   cup semi-sweet chocolate
    morsels
½   cup chopped pecans

Preheat oven to 350°. Beat first 3 ingredients at medium speed with an electric mixer until smooth. Stir in chocolate morsels and pecans. Drop by teaspoonfuls onto ungreased baking sheets. Bake for 8 to 10 minutes. Remove and cool cookies on rack.

Easy Banana Pudding

7-8 bananas, sliced
1 large box vanilla wafers
2 small boxes vanilla instant
    pudding
1 can sweetened condensed milk
1 16-ounce tub whipped topping

Blend pudding according to package directions. Add condensed milk and stir. Fold in whipped topping. Place wafers in bottom of 3-quart shallow baking dish. Alternate layers of pudding, bananas and wafers, ending with pudding. Top with whipped topping, if desired, chill and serve.

10 TO 12 SERVINGS.

* * * * * * * * * * * * * * *

Prepare 1 day in advance.

Easy Pralines

¼ cup butter
1 cup firmly packed brown sugar
⅓ cup whipping cream
1 cup confectioners' sugar
1 teaspoon vanilla extract
1 cup chopped pecans

Bring first 3 ingredients to a boil over medium heat, stirring often. Boil approximately 5 minutes, stirring constantly. Remove from heat. Whisk in 1 cup of confectioners' sugar and vanilla extract until smooth. Stir in pecans. Continue stirring until mixture begins to thicken. Spoon out onto wax paper. Cool completely on wax paper before removing.

English Tea Cakes

1 cup butter, softened	12 maraschino cherries
1 cup sugar	1 tablespoon cherry juice
2 eggs	(from cherry jar)
2 cups all-purpose flour	½ cup currants
½ teaspoon baking powder	1 jar maraschino cherries for
¼ teaspoon salt	garnishing
1 teaspoon vanilla extract	

Preheat oven to 250°. Grease and flour a Pampered Chef flower tube pan. Cream butter and sugar. Add eggs, beating thoroughly. Sift flour, baking powder and salt together. Gradually add to butter mixture. Add vanilla extract and cherry juice. Fold in cherries and raisins. Bake for 1¼ hours. Slice cake and garnish with a half cherry in the middle of the slice.

Fudge

2 cups sugar	1 6-ounce package chocolate chip
pinch of salt	morsels
1 stick of butter	1 cup chopped pecan, optional
⅔ cup pet milk	1 teaspoon vanilla extract
12 big marshmallows	

Bring sugar, salt, butter, milk and marshmallows to a boil on the stove. Turn it down and cook for 5 minutes. Add chocolate chip morsels, pecans, and vanilla extract. Pour into an 8x8-inch baking pan. Best if the fudge sits overnight at room temperature before cutting.

Frozen Hawaiian Pie

1	14-ounce can sweetened condensed milk
1	12-ounce container frozen whipped topping thawed
1	20-ounce can crushed pineapple, drained
2	tablespoons lemon juice
1/2	cup mashed ripe banana (about 1 large banana)

1	large orange, peeled and sectioned
1/2	cup sweetened flaked coconut
1/2	cup chopped walnuts, toasted
1/2	cup maraschino cherries
2	9-inch ready-made graham cracker crusts

Garnishes

chopped pineapple
maraschino cherries
chopped walnuts

whipped topping
toasted coconut
fresh mint sprigs

Stir together condensed milk and whipped topping. Fold in next 7 ingredients. Pour evenly into graham cracker crusts. Cover and freeze 12 hours or until firm. Remove from freezer, and let stand 10 minutes before serving. Garnish, if desired.

Fruit Cobbler

1/2	cup butter
1	cup self-rising flour
1	cup sugar

1	cup milk
1	pint blackberries or blueberries

Melt butter in an 8-inch pan. Mix flour and sugar in a bowl. Slowly add milk and stir. Pour over melted butter. Do not stir. Add fruit. Bake 1 hour at 300°.

Desserts

Fudge Pie

1 cup butter or margarine, softened	2 cups sugar
½ cup flour	1 cup nuts
½ cup cocoa	4 eggs

Cream butter and sugar. Add eggs one at a time and beat after each one. Sift flour and cocoa into mixture. Add nuts. Pour into lightly greased 10-inch pie plate. Bake for 25 to 30 minutes at 375° or until crust forms on top. Serve with ice cream or whipped cream.

Iced Chocolate Brownies with Coffee Liquor

Brownies

1 box fudge brownie mix	⅓ cup vegetable oil
3 eggs	

Icing

½ cup plus 6 teaspoons unsalted butter (divided use)	2 tablespoons coffee liqueur
2 cups confectioners' sugar	1¼ cups semi-sweet chocolate chips

Prepare brownies according to directions. Cool about 30 minutes. In a glass bowl, melt ½ cup butter in the microwave. Stir in confectioners' sugar and coffee liquor. Stir until smooth and spread evenly over brownies. Chill about 1 hour. In a small heatproof bowl, melt 6 tablespoons butter and chocolate chips in the microwave. Take care not to scorch. Stir until smooth and spread over frosted brownies. Chill at least 1 hour before cutting.

Desserts

German Chocolate Bundt Cake

1   package German chocolate cake mix
1   can coconut pecan frosting
4   eggs
1   cup oil

1/2   cup water
1   6-ounce package milk chocolate chips
1   cup chopped pecans

Preheat oven to 325°. Mix all ingredients together by hand, and pour into a well-greased Bundt pan. Bake for 55 to 60 minutes. Cool in pan for 20 minutes before turning out.

Gracie's Glazed Lemon Cake

1   18¼-ounce package yellow cake mix
1   ¾-ounce package instant lemon pudding mix

¾   cup oil
¾   cup water
4   eggs

Glaze

2   cups confectioners' sugar
1/3   cup lemon juice

2   tablespoons butter, melted
2   tablespoons water

Mix together all ingredients. Pour into a greased 9x13-inch pan. Bake at 350° for 35 to 40 minutes or until a toothpick inserted in center comes out clean. Remove cake from oven and immediately poke holes through the cake with a fork; combine glaze ingredients and pour over top.

10 TO 12 SERVINGS.

Desserts

Ice Cream Dessert

1 cup butter	1 jar caramel topping
½ cup brown sugar	1 jar fudge topping
2 cups flour	pecans, chopped
1 quart vanilla ice cream, softened	

Preheat oven to 350°. Mix flour and brown sugar. Cut in butter. Spread into a 9x13-inch baking dish. Cook for 10 min. COOL completely. Pour caramel topping onto crust. Spread on the ice cream. Top with chopped pecans. Freeze completely (at least 2 hours). Remove from freezer 15 minutes prior to serving. Heat fudge topping and pour over each individual serving.

Iron Skillet Upside-Down Cake

³⁄₄ cup butter	2 large eggs
2 cups sugar	1½ cups all-purpose flour
3 large Granny Smith apples, peeled and cut into ½-inch thick slices	1 teaspoon baking powder
	1 teaspoon ground cinnamon
1 cup chopped pecans	½ cup milk

Melt ¼ cup butter in skillet, medium heat. Add 1 cup sugar and cook, stirring often, 2 minutes or until sugar is melted and begins to turn golden. Add apples and cook, stirring often, 5 minutes or until apples have softened and juices are thickened and syrupy. Remove skillet from heat and sprinkle ½ cup pecans. Set aside. Beat remaining ½ cup butter until creamy. Gradually add remaining 1 cup sugar, beating until light and fluffy. Add eggs, 1 at a time. Stir flour, baking powder, and cinnamon together and add to butter mixture with milk, beating at low speed. Stir in remaining ½ cup pecans. Spoon batter evenly over apple mixture in skillet. Bake at 350° for 30 minutes. Cool in skillet 5 minutes, invert onto serving plate.

Kahlúa Cake

1	box yellow cake mix	3/4	cup water
1	large box instant chocolate pudding	4	large eggs
1	cup vegetable oil	1/4	cup Kahlúa
		1/4	cup vodka

Mix all ingredients in a large bowl. Bake in a Bundt pan for 45 to 55 minutes at 350°.

Key Lime Pie

1 1/4	cups graham cracker crumbs	1	cup Key lime juice
1/4	cup firmly packed light brown sugar	2	egg whites
1/3	cup butter, melted	1/4	teaspoon cream of tartar
2	14-ounce cans sweetened condensed milk	2	tablespoons granulated sugar

Combine first 3 ingredients. Press into a 9-inch pie plate. Bake pie crust at 350° for 10 minutes or until lightly browned. Cool. Stir together sweetened condensed milk and lime juice until blended. Pour into prepared crust. Set aside. Beat egg whites and cream of tartar at high speed with an electric mixer just until foamy. Add granulated sugar gradually, 1 tablespoon at a time, beating until soft peaks form and sugar dissolves (2 to 4 minutes). Spread meringue over filling. Bake at 325° for 25 to 28 minutes. Chill 8 hours.

Desserts

Lady Fingers

5 cups plain flour	3 cups chopped pecans
1 cup sugar	vanilla extract
1 pound butter, softened	confectioners' sugar

Cream sugar and butter. Add flour, one cup at a time, until well mixed. Add nuts. Mix well. Add vanilla extract as needed to moisten dry ingredients. When all ingredients are mixed together, put small amounts of butter in hands, pinch off small amounts of dough, and roll between hands until dough resembles your index finger. Be sure to make all fingers approximately the same size. Place on ungreased cookie sheet and bake at 350° until lightly brown. Remove lady fingers from the cookie sheet, cool, and then roll them in confectioners' sugar. Place 2 to 3 inches of confectioners' sugar in the bottom of a glass jar. After rolling lady fingers, place them in the jar and liberally sprinkle confectioners' sugar over them. Place 15 to 20 fingers in the jar. Continue doing this until jar is full.

Lemon Ice Box Pie

1 Nilla crust	1 can condensed milk
2 lemons	1 8-ounce tub whipped topping
3 egg yolks	

Beat eggs adding milk and blend. Mix in juice of lemons. Fold mixture into pie crust. Mix whipped topping until creamy, and then add to top of pie. Cool overnight and serve.

8 TO 10 SERVINGS.

• • • • • • • • • • • • • • •

Prepare 1 to 2 days prior.

Desserts

Lime Tarts

Shells

1	3-ounce package cream cheese, softened
½	cup butter, softened

1½	cups all-purpose flour
3	tablespoons pet milk
½	teaspoon vanilla extract

Combine cream cheese and butter until smooth. Add flour mixing well. Refrigerate dough for 1 hour. Shape into small balls about the size of a large marble. Put each ball in a greased miniature muffin tin shaping into a shell. Prick dough with a fork. Bake at 350° for 15 minutes.

Filling

1	15-ounce can sweetened condensed milk
¼	cup lime juice (about 4 limes)

1	cup crushed pineapple, drained (9 ounce can)
5	drops green food coloring
1	16-ounce tub whipped topping

Combine condensed milk and lime juice. Stir until thickened. Blend in drained pineapple and food coloring. Mix well. Chill until firm (preferably overnight). Fill shells with filling and dap small amount of whipped topping on top.

Desserts

Hummingbird Cake

3	cups flour	
2	cups sugar	
1	teaspoon salt	
1	teaspoon baking soda	
1	teaspoon cinnamon	
1¼	cups oil	

3	eggs, well beaten
1½	teaspoons vanilla extract
1	8-ounce can crushed pineapple
¼	cup pecans
2	cups chopped banana
¼	cup black walnuts

Preheat oven to 350°. Grease and wax paper 3 (9-inch) cake pans. Combine all dry ingredients in large mixing bowl. Add eggs and oil mixing until all is moistened. Do not beat with mixer, hand stir ingredients. Stir in vanilla extract, pineapple and nuts. Add bananas. Spoon the batter into 3 well-greased and papered cake pans. Bake in preheated oven for 25 to 30 minutes or until cake is done. Cool in pan for 10 minutes then turn on cooling rack. Cool completely before frosting.

Cream Cheese Frosting

2	8-ounce packages cream cheese, softened
1	32-ounce box confectioners' sugar

2	teaspoons vanilla extract
1	cup chopped pecans
1	cup butter at room temperature

Combine cream cheese and butter until smooth. Add sugar, beating with mixer until fluffy. Stir in vanilla extract. Frost the tops of each cake and stack. Fill circle on top with pecans.

Desserts

Italian Cream Cake

½	cup butter	1	cup buttermilk
½	cup vegetable oil	2	cups flour
2	cups sugar	1	teaspoon vanilla extract
5	eggs, separated	1	cup shredded coconut
1	teaspoon baking soda	½	cup chopped pecans

Preheat overt to 325°. Cream together butter, oil and sugar. Add egg yolks one at a time, beating well after each addition. Dissolve baking soda in buttermilk and add alternately with flour to the butter mixture. Beat egg whites until stiff and fold into the batter. Add vanilla extract, coconut and pecans: mix well. Pour into 3 greased and floured 8-inch or 9-inch layer cake pans. Bake for approximately 25 minutes. When cool, ice with cream cheese pecan icing

Cream Cheese Pecan Icing

2	8-ounce packages cream cheese	2	teaspoons vanilla extract
1	cup butter, softened	2	pounds confectioners' sugar
1	cup chopped pecans		

Mix all ingredients until creamy.

Madame Benoit's Chocolate Pots De Crème

1　cup semi-sweet chocolate pieces
3　tablespoons strong coffee
2　tablespoons coffee liqueur
2　eggs

²/₃　cup light cream heated just to boiling
sweetened whipped cream
chocolate curls

In a blender, combine chocolate pieces, coffee, coffee liqueur, eggs, and heated cream. Cover and blend at high speed for 3 minutes. Pour into custard cups. Chill at least 4 hours. Top with whipped cream. Garnish with chocolate curls.

Melting Moments

1　cup butter
1　cup all-purpose flour

¹/₃　cup confectioners' sugar
²/₃　cup cornstarch

Place butter in mixer to cream. Gradually add flour, sugar, and cornstarch. Dust hands with confectioners' sugar and roll into 1-inch balls. Drop on ungreased cookie sheet. Bake 10 to 15 minutes at 325°. Cookies will be light brown on bottom only! This recipe should yield 50 to 60 cookies. If it doesn't, the cookie balls are too large and you need to make them smaller. Once cookies are done, ICE THEM IMMEDIATELY. The icing will melt over them. FYI, these cookies are fragile, handle with care.

Icing

¹/₄　cup butter, NOT MARGARINE
2　cups confectioners' sugar

2　tablespoons lemon juice

Cream butter and sugar in electric mixer. Add lemon juice. Use a scant ½ teaspoon to ice cookies. You need them to have a glazed look so YOU MUST ICE THEM WHILE THEY'RE HOT!!!

Desserts

Meringue Cookies

2   eggs, whites only
2/3 cup sugar
1   teaspoon vanilla extract

1   6-ounce package semi-sweet
    chocolate chips

Preheat over to 250°. Beat egg white until stiff. Add sugar gradually. Add vanilla extract. Fold in chocolate chips. Drop teaspoon full of batter on foil-lined cookie sheet. Place cookies into oven and turn the oven off, leave in overnight.

3 DOZEN.

• • • • • • • • • • • • • • •

Preparation time: overnight.

Microwave Fudge

1   16-ounce box light brown sugar
2   tablespoons light corn syrup
1   cup whipping cream

1   tablespoon butter
2   cups chopped pecans

Combine brown sugar, corn syrup, and whipping cream in large microwave safe bowl. Cook in microwave on high for 13 minutes. Add butter and pecans. Beat candy mixture until creamy. Drop by teaspoons onto waxed paper or pour into 8x8x2-inch buttered pan and cut into squares.

Millionaire Pie

1	graham cracker crust	1	can crushed pineapple, drained
1	can condensed milk	1	tub whipped topping
¼	cup lemon juice	1	cup pecans

Mix all of the ingredients together, place into the graham cracker crust. Refrigerate for 2 to 3 hours prior to serving.

8 TO 10 SERVINGS.

Mom's Caramel Brownies

1	14-ounce package caramels, unwrapped	⅔	cup butter, melted
⅔	cup evaporated milk, divided	1	cup chopped pecans
1	18¼-ounce package German chocolate cake mix	1	12-ounce package chocolate chips

Combine caramels and ⅓ cup evaporated milk in a microwave-safe bowl. Heat, stirring occasionally until caramels have melted. Set aside. Combine cake mix, butter, remaining ⅓ cup evaporated milk and pecans. Press half of cake mixture into bottom of greased and floured 9x13-inch baking pan. Bake at 350° for 8 minutes. Remove from oven. Sprinkle with chocolate chips and spread caramel mixture over the top. Drop remaining cake mixture by spoonfuls on top of caramel mixture and bake an additional 15 to 18 minutes. Cool slightly. Refrigerate 30 minutes to firm caramel layer. Cut into bars.

2 DOZEN.

Mississippi Mud Cake

2 sticks butter or margarine	1 cup chopped nuts
2 cups sugar	1 teaspoon vanilla extract
¼ cup cocoa	1 small can flaked coconut
4 large eggs	1 pint marshmallow cream
1½ cups flour	cocoa frosting

Melt butter in a saucepan over low heat. Remove from heat. Add sugar and cocoa. Beat with a hand-held mixer until creamy. Add eggs, 1 at a time, beating well after each addition. Add flour, beating well. Stir nuts, vanilla extract, and coconut. Pour batter into a greased and floured 13x9-inch baking dish. Bake at 350° for 40 to 45 minutes. Remove from oven and spread immediately with marshmallow cream. Cool completely on a wire rack. Spread with frosting.

Cocoa Frosting

½ cup butter or margarine	1 pound confectioners' sugar
⅓ cup cocoa	2 teaspoons vanilla extract
¼ cup evaporated milk	

Melt margarine in a saucepan. Add cocoa, milk, and sugar, and beat with a hand-held mixer until smooth. Remove from heat. Add vanilla extract, beating well.

Desserts

Orange Cookies

1	cup sugar	2	cups self-rising flour
1	cup brown sugar	2	cups oatmeal
3/4	cup vegetable oil	1¼	cups finely chopped orange slice candy
2	eggs		
1	teaspoon vanilla extract		

Preheat oven to 350°. In a large bowl, mix sugar, brown sugar and vegetable oil together until well blended. Add eggs and vanilla extract, mixing well. Stir in flour and oatmeal. Add orange slice candy pieces. Drop by teaspoons 2 inches apart on an ungreased baking sheet. Bake 10 to 12 minutes. Cool on baking sheet for 3 minutes. Place on wire rack to cool completely.

4 DOZEN.

Pecan Pie

½	cup sugar	1	teaspoon vanilla extract
3	tablespoons butter	1	cup white syrup
2	eggs, beaten	2	cups chopped pecans
2	tablespoons flour	1	unbaked pie shell
¼	teaspoon salt		

Cream sugar and butter. Add beaten eggs. Add flour, salt, vanilla and syrup. Mix well and add pecans. Pour into pie crust and bake at 385° for 35 to 45 minutes until firm in the middle.

Pear Pie with Crumb Topping

1 pound peeled, sliced and cored pears (about 4 pears)
½ cup sugar
1 teaspoon grated lemon peel

3 tablespoons lemon juice
3 tablespoons flour
1 unbaked, deep dish pie shell

Crumb Topping

½ cup flour
½ cup sugar
½ teaspoon mace
½ teaspoon ginger

½ teaspoon cinnamon
4 tablespoons butter, soften but not melted

Mix above ingredients well and spread over pear filling.

Preheat oven to 400°. Pour lemon juice over pear slices. Mix together lemon peel, sugar and flour. Mix with pear slices and lemon juice. Arrange pear slices in bottom of unbaked pie shell. Top with crumb topping. Bake in 400° oven for 45 minutes or until pears are tender and pie is brown.

Peanut Butter Pie

½ cup peanut butter
1 can condensed milk

3 cups whipped topping
1 graham cracker crust

Mix peanut butter and condensed milk until well blended. Fold whipped topping into mixture and pour into pie shell. Refrigerate until hard.

● ● ● ● ● ● ● ● ● ● ● ● ● ●

Whipped topping can also be added to top when served.

Desserts

Pecan Pie Muffins

1	cup chopped pecans	2	large eggs
1	cup firmly packed brown sugar	1/2	cup butter or margarine, melted
1/2	cup all-purpose flour		

Combine first 3 ingredients in a large bowl. Make a well in center of mixture. Beat eggs until foamy. Stir together eggs and butter. Add to dry ingredients, stirring until moistened. Place foil baking cups in muffin pans and coat with cooking spray. Spoon batter into cups, filling 2/3 full. Bake at 350° for 20 to 25 minutes or until done. Remove from pans immediately. Cool on wire racks.

9 MUFFINS.

Potato Chip Cookies

1	pound butter	2	cups crushed potato chips (not Ruffles)
1	cup sugar		
1	teaspoon vanilla extract	1/2	cup chopped pecans, optional
3 1/2	cups flour		confectioners' sugar (for dusting)

Preheat oven to 350°. Cream butter and sugar. Add vanilla extract. Stir in flour. Add potato chips and nuts. Drop teaspoon size cookies on ungreased cookie sheet. (These can be spaced close together on a cookie sheet as they don't spread much.) Bake approximately 15 minutes or until just turning slightly brown. Cookies will be light in color. Do not over bake. Remove from oven and dust with confectioners' sugar.

10 DOZEN.

• • • • • • • • • • • • • • • • • •

Can be cut in half.

Desserts

Pecan Tassies

1   pie crust (the kind wrapped in
    plastic that unfolds)
2   tablespoon butter or margarine,
    melted

3/4   cup firmly packed brown sugar
1   egg
1   teaspoon vanilla extract
1½   cups chopped pecans

Preheat oven to 350°. Roll out dough to make it a little thinner. Cut out circles
with a biscuit cutter or scalloped edge cookie cutter and place in an ungreased
MINI muffin pan. Combine filling ingredients together and fill each tin evenly.
Bake 20 to 25 minutes or until light golden brown. Remove to cool.

Pound Cake

3   cups all-purpose flour
4   cups sugar
1   pound butter, softened

3/4   cup whole milk
6   eggs
2   teaspoons vanilla extract

Place flour, sugar, butter, milk, eggs and vanilla extract (in that order) in a
4-quart mixing bowl. Beat at low speed for 1 minute. Scrape down sides and beat
at medium speed for 2 minutes. Pour in a greased and floured tube pan. Bake
at 325° for 1½ hours or until a wooden pick comes out clean. Cool in pan on a
wire rack for 10 minutes. Remove from pan. Cool completely on a wire rack.

Desserts

Pumpkin Cheesecake

3	8-ounce packages cream cheese, softened	2	eggs
1	cup sugar	1	5-ounce can evaporated milk
1/4	cup light brown sugar, packed	2	tablespoons cornstarch
1	16-ounce can solid pack pumpkin	1 1/4	teaspoons ground cinnamon
		1/2	teaspoon ground nutmeg

Topping

2	cups sour cream	1	teaspoon vanilla extract
1/4-1/3	cup sugar		

Crust

Combine graham cracker crumbs, sugar and butter in medium bowl. Press onto bottom of 9-inch springform pan and 1-inch up side. Bake in preheated 350° oven for 6 to 8 minutes. Do not allow to brown. Remove from oven and cool.

Cheesecake

Beat cream cheese, sugar and brown sugar in large mixer until fluffy. Beat in pumpkin, eggs and evaporated milk. Add cornstarch, cinnamon and nutmeg. Beat well. Pour into crust. Bake at 350° for 50 to 60 minutes or until edge is set.

Topping

Combine sour cream, sugar and vanilla extract in a small bowl. Spread over surface of warm cheesecake. Return to 350° oven and back 5 minutes. Cool on wire rack. Remove side of pan. Chill several hours or overnight.

Pumpkin Crunch

1	16-ounce can solid pack pumpkin	1/2	teaspoon salt
1	12-ounce can evaporated milk	1	package yellow cake mix
3	eggs	1	cup chopped pecans
1 1/2	cups sugar	1	cup melted margarine or butter
4	teaspoons pumpkin pie spice		

Preheat oven to 350°. Grease bottom only of a 9x13-inch pan. Mix first 6 ingredients until smooth. Pour into pan. Sprinkle dry cake mix evenly over the top of pumpkin mixture. Spread pecan pieces over that and drizzle melted butter over all. Bake 50 to 60 minutes.

Raspberry Chocolate Chip Loaf

3	8-ounce packages cream cheese, softened	1	tablespoon ground cinnamon
1/2	cup chopped pecans	1	cup confectioners' sugar
1	cup raspberry chocolate chips	1	plain chocolate bar

Melt 1/3 cup chips and add to cream cheese and confectioners' sugar. Beat well. Stir in rest of chips and cinnamon. Put in mold lined with plastic wrap. Chill overnight. Top with chopped pecans and grated chocolate bar before serving. Serve with cinnamon sticks, gingersnaps, or strawberries.

Desserts

Red Velvet Cake

½ cup shortening	2 teaspoons cocoa
1½ cups sugar	1 cup buttermilk
2 large eggs	1 tablespoon white vinegar
1-2 1-ounce bottles red food coloring	1 teaspoon baking soda
1 teaspoon vanilla extract	cream cheese frosting
2½ cups sifted cake flour	garnish with chopped pecans
½ teaspoon salt	

Beat shortening at medium speed with an electric mixer until fluffy. Gradually add sugar, beating well. Add eggs, 1 at a time, beating until blended after each addition. Stir in food coloring and vanilla extract, blending well. Combine flour, salt and cocoa. Set aside. Combine buttermilk, vinegar, and soda in a 4 cup liquid measuring cup. Mixture will bubble. Add flour mixture to shortening mixture, alternate with buttermilk mixture, beginning and ending with the flour mixture. Beat at low speed until blended after each addition. Beat at medium speed 2 minutes. Pour batter into 3 greased and floured 8-inch round cake pans. Bake at 350° for 25 minutes. Cool in pans on wire racks 10 minutes. Remove from pans and cool completely on wire racks. Spread cream cheese frosting between layers and on top of cake. If desired, garnish with chopped pecans.

Cream Cheese Frosting

1 8-ounce package cream cheese, softened	1 16-ounce package confectioners' sugar
½ cup butter or margarine, softened	1 teaspoon vanilla extract

Beat cream cheese and butter until fluffy. Gradually add confectioners' sugar, beating at low speed until blended. Add vanilla extract beating until blended

Shortbread

3   cups flour
1½ cups butter, no margarine

1   cup confectioners' sugar

Cream butter and sugar. Add flour. Press into an ungreased 9x13-inch pan. Bake at 300° for 40 minutes. Cut with sharp knife while hot (in pan) into 1-inch squares.

Snickerdoodle Cookies

2   tablespoons sugar
2   teaspoons ground cinnamon
½ cup margarine, softened
1½ cups sugar
2   large eggs

2¾ cups all-purpose flour
2   teaspoons cream of tartar
1   teaspoon baking soda
¼ teaspoon salt

Stir together 2 tablespoons sugar and cinnamon and set aside. Beat margarine and 1½ cups sugar at medium speed with an electric mixer until creamy. Add eggs, 1 at a time, beating just until blended after each addition. Combine flour and next 3 ingredients. Gradually add to sugar mixture, beating until blended. Shape dough into 1-inch balls. Roll in cinnamon-sugar mixture. Place 2 inches apart on an aluminum foil-lined baking sheet. Bake at 350°, in batches, 8 to 10 minutes or until lightly browned. Transfer to wire racks to cool.

Desserts

Snickers Pie

4	king-sized Snicker bars	1	deep dish 9-inch graham cracker pie crust
½	cup peanut butter		Additional whipped topping and Hershey's chocolate syrup for garnish
1½	tablespoons half-and-half		
4	cups frozen whipped topping, thawed		

In the top of a double boiler, melt together Snickers bars, peanut butter, and half-and-half, stirring until smooth. Remove from heat and allow to cool slightly. Fold in whipped topping. Pour into crust and freeze for 4 to 6 hours before serving. When ready to serve, top with additional whipped topping and drizzle with Hershey's chocolate syrup. Store in refrigerator.

6 TO 8 SERVINGS.

Strawberry Cake

1	box yellow or white cake mix	1	teaspoon vanilla extract
1	3-ounce box strawberry gelatin	1	10-ounce package frozen strawberries, thawed
4	eggs		
1	cup oil	1	cup margarine, softened
3	tablespoons flour	1	box confectioners' sugar
½	cup water		

Preheat oven to 350°. Cake: mix cake mix, eggs, gelatin, oil, water, flour, and vanilla extract until smooth. Add strawberries, saving ½ cup. Beat until strawberries are in pieces. Bake in 3 layers for 25 to 30 minutes. (May also be baked in a 9x13-inch baking dish.)

Icing: Cream the margarine and confectioners' sugar. Add the remaining ½ cup of strawberries. Add water as needed, being careful not to make it too thin.

Strawberry Cheesecake

Crust

2   sticks butter

2   cups sifted flour

2   tablespoons sugar

1   cup chopped pecans

Melt butter in bowl. Remove from heat. Add sugar and flour. Mix well. Press evenly into 9x13-inch pan. Bake 350° for 15 to 20 minutes.

Filling

3   8-ounce packages cream cheese

1   12-ounce container whipped topping

1   teaspoon vanilla extract

3   cups confectioners' sugar

2-3 cups chopped strawberries (add to taste)

Blend cream cheese, sugar, 8-ounces of whipped topping, and vanilla extract in bowl until very smooth. Completely cool the crust then spread the filling on top of the crust. Spread the strawberries on top of filling. Refrigerate for at least 4 hours or overnight. Spread the rest of the whipped topping on top when ready to serve.

Strawberry Nut Bread

1½ cups vegetable oil
4 eggs, beaten
2 cups sugar
1 teaspoon salt
3 cups plain flour

1 teaspoon baking soda
4 teaspoons cinnamon
2 pints fresh strawberries, chopped
1 cup chopped pecans

Cream together oil, eggs and sugar. Mix in salt, flour, soda and cinnamon. Stir in strawberries and pecans. Pour into 2 greased and floured 9x5-inch loaf pans. Bake at 400° for 1 hour and 10 minutes.

Three Berry Cobbler

1 12-ounce package frozen blackberries, unthawed
1 12-ounce package frozen raspberries, unthawed
1 12-ounce package frozen blueberries, unthawed
1½ cups sugar

½ cup all-purpose flour
¼ cup butter or margarine, melted
1 teaspoon vanilla extract
1 15-ounce package refrigerated pie crust
1 large egg, lightly beaten
1 tablespoon sugar

Stir together first 7 ingredients in a large bowl, stirring just until combined. Spoon into a lightly greased 9x13-inch baking dish. Roll 1 pie crust to fit baking dish. Place on top of berry mixture. Cut remaining pie crust into ½-inch strips. Arrange strips in a lattice design over pie crust. Brush with egg and lightly sprinkle with 1 tablespoon sugar. Bake at 400° for 55 to 60 minutes or until golden and bubbly.

Desserts

Sweet Potato Pie

2	medium cans yams, mashed	3	eggs
1½	cans condensed milk	1	stick butter
1	cup sugar	2	unbaked pie shells
1	teaspoon vanilla extract		

Mix and pour into pie shells. Bake at 350° for about 1 hour.

Yam Delight

Crust

| ¾ | cup flour | 1 | cup chopped pecans |
| 1¾ | sticks butter | ¼ | teaspoon vanilla |

Mix well and press into a 9x13-inch buttered casserole dish. Bake at 350° for 30 minutes or until light golden brown. Remove from oven and cool.

Yams
4 large red yams

Boil yams until soft. Drain and peel while hot and beat in a mixer until creamy. Fiber will cling to mixer. Cool.

Filling

1	cup milk	1	cup confectioners' sugar
1	large box vanilla instant pudding		6-ounces whipped topping
1	8-ounce package cream cheese		

In a mixing bowl combine milk and pudding. Add to cooled yams. Beat together remaining ingredients. When crust is cool, spread cream cheese mixture on top of crust. Then spread yam pudding mixture on top of cream cheese layer. Cover top with remaining half of cool whip and sprinkle with finely chopped pecans. Refrigerate for 30 minutes.

Desserts

Turtle Cake

1	14-ounce package caramels	1	cup chocolate chips
3/4	cup margarine, melted	1	box German chocolate cake mix
2/3	cup evaporated milk	1	cup chopped pecans

Combine caramels and 1/3 cup evaporated milk. Cook over low heat until caramels are melted, stirring constantly. Set aside. Combine dry cake mix, margarine, nuts, and 1/3 cup evaporated milk. Stir by hand until dough holds together. Press 2/3 of dough into a 9x13-inch pan that has been greased and floured. Bake at 350° for 6 minutes. Remove from oven. Spread caramel mixture over top. Sprinkle chocolate chips over top of caramel. Crumble remaining mixture of cake on top. Bake 15 to 18 additional minutes. Dough may appear not to be thoroughly cooked but should be soft and chewy. Cool and cut into squares.

Vanilla Pears

3	15-ounce cans chopped pears, undrained	1/3	cup sugar
2	tablespoons cornstarch	2	tablespoons bourbon
1	teaspoon vanilla extract	2	tablespoons butter
1/4	teaspoon ground cinnamon	1/4	cup chopped toasted pecans

Drain pears reserving 1 1/4 cups liquid. Set pears aside. Combine 1/4 cup reserved liquid with cornstarch, vanilla extract, and cinnamon, stirring until smooth. Combine remaining 1 cup liquid with sugar, bourbon and butter in a small saucepan. Gradually stir in cornstarch mixture. Cook over low heat, stirring constantly, until butter melts and sauce is thickened. Place pears in an ungreased 8-inch baking dish. Pour sauce over pears and sprinkle with pecans. Bake uncovered at 350° for 18 minutes until bubbly.

6 SERVINGS.

• • • • • • • • • • • • • • •

Serve warm. This can be used as is or it can be drizzled over ice cream or pound cake.

Desserts

Notes

Notes

Index

Index

Index

Index

Index

Index

Index

Index

Index

Index

Notes

Notes